Copyright Page 2025 by Felisha Fowler Taylor

ISBN: 979-8-9925266-7-7

No part of this publication may be reproduced, stored in a retrieval system or transmitted in any way by any means, electronic, mechanical, photocopy, recording or otherwise without proper permission of the author except as provided by USA copyright law.

Editor: Yolanda R. Toney, Ed.D. (Writeously Correct LLC.)

www.writeouslycorrect.com

Formatted by: Merisha Ford (M3 Designs & Marketing)

Special thanks to Clay McCombs for preliminary book review.

ISBN: 979-8-9925266-7-7

Dedication

I dedicate this book to my loving mom and sons who encouraged me to write a book, so I can use the challenges of my life and turn them into dreams, so others can as well.

Acknowledgments

Thank you to my Lord and Savior, Jesus Christ, who carried me through the darkest valley of my life. He is the lifter of my head and everlasting joy in my heart. May every reader come to know Him and love Him more deeply.

I would like to give a sincere thanks to my family, friends, and colleagues who came alongside with calls, texts, gems of wisdom, and abundant unconditional love.

Thank you to Dr. Barbara Neely who invested her time and energy in me when she did not even know me. I thank her for her time, love, and connections that have inspired me to believe in myself and to become an author.

Preface

First, let me begin by saying, I do not advocate divorce. Let me repeat that again; I do not advocate divorce. However, there is a time perhaps when a relationship has become toxic and you need to shed an old skin just like an animal shed its fur in the winter and a snake sheds its skin, so something can grow and be healthy and flourish. I've written this book with that very idea to help you shed the pain, the trauma, the parts of you that need to be healed and regenerate the parts of you that must become new. There are even parts like boundaries that may have been there all along when you just don't know what you haven't been taught, and that's okay. I'm here to guide you, to help you, and to love you through this process, so you can get out on the other side where life is better than ever.

Love you,
Felisha

Introduction

We are headed to the other side. "The other side" was the repeated words spoken to me over and over again. It began shortly after my separation and headed towards my divorce which became final on November 30, 2021. It was a devastating end to a relationship with my childhood sweetheart. The first time I heard that phrase was with a complete stranger. I quickly changed my benefactors to my children on my retirement plan. Certainly, if I were going to die anytime soon, *he* would not benefit from it one cent. I was hurt, angry, scared, and vigilant to protect my children any way I could.

As I spoke to the customer service representative over the phone to get details on how to begin that process, I told her my circumstances. You see, I am often an open book…hence, my need to write it all down and pass it along to you. Call it a gift or perhaps a curse. I have found healing in speaking, but I have also found much pain in it as well. Nonetheless, we all operate as we are built.

The lady, on the other end, shared with me her experience with divorce too. She calmly said, "I understand. It is hard, but it is better on the other side of it." Those words planted a little seed of hope within me that day. In the middle of the worst emotional pain that I had ever been in, her seed was lifesaving. Words are seeds. Something always grows from them.

Here is the thing about emotional pain - your mind does not know the difference between it and physical pain. Pain is pain. Often, it is the emotional pain that does not heal as soon. Unlike a physical injury, emotional trauma cannot be seen. Therefore, there is not the same amount of care to the one impacted by emotional trauma. In fact, you are told uncertain things like "get over it, move on, and it is ok." Even though people mean well, they unintentionally cause more emotional pain. Afterwards, you find yourself more isolated and unable to express your pain in a safe place. Your therapist can even upset you with his/her seeming words of wisdom. People do not mean harm, but sometimes they cause it unknowingly. I, too, being human, have made the exact same mistakes.

This book may trigger you. However, it is written to heal you. Forgive me up front when you are triggered, for I do not mean you harm. I mean to bless you and not curse you as the Father would have me to do. The only way to the other side, however, is through the valley of pain. You will cry. You will get angry. You will also smile, and I know God has plans to prosper you and not harm you just like His word says. When you cannot figure out what to believe, believe His word. It does not change. It is life changing. His word is a trustworthy roadmap you can rely on. It will bring you closer to Him and the other side.

Close your eyes and imagine what you desire for the other side to look like. There's peace (emotional, mental and financial), safety, real love, acceptance of others and yourself, and more understanding of the trial. The other side is beautiful! It is not perfect. Only heaven is that, but it is a good place to be. When I was breaking and giving up hope, people would pray with me and say in the prayer, "the other side." I heard those three words in sermons and songs, and it was just undeniable; it was God speaking. He was saying, "write, say it, believe it." Let's go to the other side together.

Rules For The Road

Before you set out on this road, you need to have clear vision. Otherwise, you will not be able to see where you are going. The rear-view mirror is there to help you see what is behind you, so you can adjust before you get over into the next lane, but you only need to glance at it ever so often. The rear-view mirror is small, but your windshield is big. What is ahead of you, your future, needs most of your attention and focus if you are going to get where you are going. Therefore, remember this along our ride together. When you feel tempted to keep looking back at your past, as you will as I have, because it is part of the journey, stay focused on what is ahead. We are going to The Other Side. I am here to ride shotgun and help you navigate this difficult terrain. There are lots of hills, valleys, curves, and bumps, and we will get caught in some difficult weather, too. It will rain, snow, and even ice, and we might slide along the road.

Rest assured though as you get tired; I will turn up the radio and find our favorite songs to sing along to. I will roll down the windows as we hang our arms out and wave them up and down with the wind. It will be like your favorite springtime day along the way. The sun will shine so brightly you will need to put your shades on. Birds will chirp. Breezes will blow. I promise you. We will have moments of sheer bliss. Just hang in there with me. So...here we go, you and me, with Jesus. Off to the other side, together!

Daily Dose - Pack Your Medicine

I believe scripture is medicine. It provides healing in a multitude of ways. Just like we take prescriptions to feel well, his word should be taken as "pray-scriptures." I'm not saying go toss your medicine bottles, but I am saying don't forsake the power of God's words. In fact, all words have power.

"Death and life are in the power of the tongue"
(Proverbs 18:31 KJV).

I recall one day, after a doctor appointment in the process of my divorce, I stopped by TJ Maxx. Right there in the middle of the store, a tsunami wave of sadness and depression flooded me. Of all places, where retail therapy generally gives me a dopamine hit equal to cocaine or some illegal drug, I fortunately have never tried, the clothing rack that had always lifted my spirits, wasn't doing a thing for me that day. In fact, I was sheepishly hanging my head down, choking back tears, sniffling and trying to hide the fact that I was losing it…right then and right there. Suddenly, a number of scriptures came to mind and to not appear completely crazy, I began saying them out loud, but only under my breath at a very low level. When I would finish saying one, another came to mind and then another. Before I knew it, I had spouted off at least 8 verses. I didn't even realize I had memorized so many that were specific to combat the emotions I was feeling at that time. I know God helped bring those verses to my memory. After I had recited them to myself, my sadness left me. Perhaps, it would be more appropriate to say my sadness ran like hell and my mood shifted from near breakdown to peace, calm and even joy before I left that store. My thoughts were clear and I could focus on the now; the enjoyment of shopping, the sun that was shining that day. I even left there and had a bite to eat at a restaurant that I had never visited before. Sitting alone didn't tear me up either.

My experience is only a tiny bit of evidence of the power of spoken scripture. With this in mind, each day in this devotional begins with a Daily Dose. I encourage you to read it aloud and believe in the power God's words possess. After all, it was what God *said* that called the whole world into existence and gave order and form to it.

Not Alone

Daily Dose
*"If either of them falls down, one can help the other up.
But pity anyone who falls and has no one to help them up."*
Ecclesiastes 4:10 (NIV)

"Woe to him that falleth when he is alone." This is one of my favorite Bible verses. The main thing I want you to know is that you are not alone. Whether you are in the "throws" of a breakup or near the end of a tragedy and feel devastated, or you feel relieved to find yourself in this new place of life as a divorcee, I want you to know without a doubt that you are not alone. That is why I chose to write this devotional. As I found myself in a divorce after 23 years of marriage to my high school sweetheart, a sudden and abrupt ending made my heart feel as if it was aching from the breakup at times. *Did I see it coming? Was there someone else? Am I not enough? What more could I have done? Who am I now? Who do I want to be? Will my children's pain end? How do I parent them through this mess? How do I move on; how do I get up? How God; how?*

The questions never end. I am here to tell you I have asked all of those and more, and I can tell you for sure, God is with you. He is closer than you can imagine if you let Him be. Some of the best advice I received upon going to church after we told our boys about the divorce was the devil wants you to follow him, but so does God - choose God; do not listen to the devil. It opened my eyes very wide. I saw with my spiritual eyes more than ever before. The devil does not want you to read this devotional during your burning pain, anger, and hurt. He wants you to wallow in sadness, depression, and grief and seek refuge in sin. You will know when he shows up tempting you to curse every day, lie, be greedy, drink to avoid the pain, and find pleasure in seeking attention and compliments. Call out the enemy and then immerse, and I do mean immerse yourself and focus on each day's principles of God's blessings. Guess what? He will show up, and He will amaze you how He shows up. He will create new Godly connections and reveal the kindness of old friends who are there for you and who show up for you over and over without judgement.

Having what is deemed as a "failed marriage" can feel very shaming, and that is even when you've done nothing to create the circumstance. Religious people can sometimes be the worst at casting you out and making you feel even more alone. Guilt and shame are not from God! He wants to draw you closer, not push you away. During my divorce, God connected me with other believers in Divorce Care class at my church. Other longtime friends came back into my life suddenly and shared with me their experience with divorce and how God had brought them through it to the other side. Some of my friends and family would call and check in on me routinely just to see how I was doing. God will supply what you need. You just have to look for it.

Day 1

List friends, family, coworkers, and others in your community who can help you. Choose wisely.

_____
_____
_____
_____
_____
_____
_____
_____
_____
_____

Give yourself the gift of gratitude.
What are you grateful for today?

_____
_____
_____
_____
_____
_____
_____
_____
_____
_____

Together

Daily Dose

"Though one may be overpowered, two can defend themselves. A cord of three strands is not quickly broken."

Ecclesiastes 4:12 (NIV)

Begin each day with prayer and read His word. This devotional is devised to help you do just that. It is sweet and simple, so you do not have to overthink and complicate it. I know how exhausted you are emotionally and mentally. Many days you cry, and there are many difficult days and nights ahead, but you are not alone on this journey. This book serves as a guide to remind you that we are walking together. My grandmother, who is also divorced, taught me a simple prayer that has helped me through this journey. Whenever you feel alone, hold your hands together and bind them, close your eyes, and pray to God. Begin the prayer with "Together, (input whatever you need here and end with Together." That's it! For instance, if you cannot find your keys one day, say, "Together, find, together." Imagine during that moment you are holding God's hand as you hold your own and sure enough, He is with you. It gives me a sense of peace, and it is a physical reminder of God's presence and knowing He is truly with me. Even the lilies of the valley are clothed in splendor because of God's love. How much more does He love you?

Day 2

Write out your prayer to God. Tell Him what your requests are here. He is listening and sees you.

_____
_____
_____
_____
_____
_____
_____
_____
_____
_____
_____
_____
_____
_____

Today, I'm grateful for:

_____
_____
_____
_____
_____
_____
_____
_____
_____
_____
_____
_____
_____
_____

Road Trip

Daily Dose
"If it seems advisable for me to go also, they will accompany me."
1 Corinthians 16:4 (NIV)

This book is designed to take you on a road trip. Imagine as we go through this complicated process together, that each day we are in a car. Some days, you drive; some days, I will be driving. Either way, we are in it together. Like all road trips, we will have plenty to talk about and discuss. We will play music, sing, and even dance sometimes. Always remember though that we are headed somewhere that we want to be. That place is The Other Side. It is the other side of our pain, deepest sadness, depression, despair, confusion, uncertainty, grief, anger, and bitterness. The Other Side is a place of joy and contentment, peace, and assurance. You are going to be, believe it or not, even better than before. Things may get bumpy, even scary at times, out there on the road, so buckle up and pay attention. I got shotgun; let's roll.

Day 3

Where do you see your life in a year from now? How might God surprise you? It is okay to dream again.
He is here and around the corner.

_____
_____
_____
_____
_____
_____
_____
_____
_____
_____
_____
_____
_____
_____
_____
_____
_____

I am grateful for these places I like to visit:

_____
_____
_____
_____
_____
_____
_____
_____
_____
_____

Rules of the Road

Daily Dose

*"For my thoughts are not your thoughts,
neither are your ways my ways,
declares the LORD."*

Isaiah 55:8 (NIV)

When you go over the speed limit, you will likely get pulled over. Even if you are fortunate enough to just get a warning, the infamous twirling red/blue lights in your rearview mirror are enough to give you a severe anxiety attack. Therefore, we will set out on this journey intending to obey the road rules. We will plan to stop at red lights, slow down at yellow ones, and put our blinkers on before we turn. Our intent is to get to the other side safely intact emotionally, mentally, and spiritually.

It is with God's laws that all the world operates, whether we acknowledge them or not, and just when we think we have escaped them, they seem to catch up. I will present some of these laws here in the upcoming days ahead, and when we get to them, please keep in mind they are there to keep us safe just like all laws. When we rush through the red lights, not slowing down at the yellow light warning us of oncoming traffic, we endanger ourselves and our lives and others. Thus, there is no skipping ahead and no rushing this thing. Our intent is to get to the other side safely intact emotionally, mentally, and spiritually. Some places will be especially hard, depending on your circumstances and wounds you have experienced. It is ok if you need to stay put at the red light a little longer. For some spots along my way, I had to get out the car, call for a taxi and then an ambulance to get me! I was severely injured there! It is okay! You may enlist all the help you need to get to the other side. Community is God's family. I pray God places you in the right community to help you on this journey. Buckle up.

Day 4

God's law is there to protect us. Often people think of the Ten Commandments. Can you lean on anyone to help you now?

I am grateful for:

Playlist

Daily Dose

*"Sing to him, sing praise to him;
tell of all his wonderful acts."*

1 Chronicles 16:9 (NIV)

We are cruising down the open highway with the wind in our hair and the sun on our faces and our favorite song turned up all the way. There is no road trip without music, so turn it up. Start singing. Play keyboards on the dashboard; play air guitar on the steering wheel. One of my favorite evangelists is Joyce Meyer. There was a particular sermon that Joyce delivered where she spoke of a certain tribe that was poor, but they were always joyful and happy, and depression was very rare among them. Part of their tradition includes singing daily and throughout the day. She mentioned they sang all the time. She joked that we, too, should try this tactic. Sing everything! Sing everyday phrases even if they are negative ones, and you will cheer up simply because of how silly you sound singing it. Imagine you're stuck in traffic, and you belt out into song, singing, *"This stupid traffic is so bad; I'm really frustrated…"* You will instantly have to chuckle at a minimum on the inside if not right out loud. Now, imagine if you can muster up a "Hallelujah" or a simple "Amen" giving praise to God. What might those words of praise do? How might you find yourself lifted and suddenly a bit hopeful?

Day 5

What are some of your favorite songs? Write them here and create an upbeat playlist. Sing along.

_____
_____
_____
_____
_____
_____
_____
_____
_____
_____

Here are a few of mine if you want to check them out:
"Good Day for a Good Day"
"Brighter Day"
 both by Michael Franti & Spearhead
"Movin' On" by Johnathan McReynolds

Something good that happened to me this week was:

_____
_____
_____
_____
_____
_____
_____

Dance

Daily Dose

"Wearing a linen ephod, David was dancing before the LORD with all his might."

2 Samuel 6:14 (NIV)

Dance like David danced. Now, I don't know about you, but I love to dance, so this one is easy; well, I thought it would be. However, it's not as easy when depression, hurt, and anger are dancing with you. It's easy to dance when you feel happiness, joy, and peace. We can easily hop up, jump around, do a two-step and electric slide, bunny hop, and shoot, even back flip then. Nevertheless, here's the thing about movement---inertia. Yes, *inertia*: an object in motion stays in motion and an object at rest; it just sits there. Movement moves you. By moving your body, you are telling your emotions to move, to shift. You don't often feel like it at first, but after that simple act of standing up, you put one foot in front of the other, and then you just step to the beat. Don't worry if you don't have rhythm. Just move, jump, anything to shift the atmosphere. Music is truly medicine. I've always known it, but more than ever now.

For instance, I had a particularly bad week. I fell into a ridiculously hard, deep low depression. I often cried every day if not every single day, but this week was different. It felt as if I was walking in mud, and the day was extremely laborious to get through. After work, I wanted nothing more than to hit the couch, cry, and sleep. I was on repeat: wake, cry, sleep. I was ashamed to tell anyone how bad it was, and I surely didn't want my son to see or be affected by my dysfunction, so I stored it up for when he or anyone else wasn't around, but just me and Jesus. We would sit there in sadness and process it, so I called it. It was therapeutic for a moment, but then I knew I was getting stuck, and now the mud I was walking in had turned into quicksand. It was dragging me deeper as I felt more shame and couldn't share it with anyone. You know when people ask that question: How ya doing? Well, I'm not a good liar. My responses were: "Well, I'm hanging." Yep, and I was hanging by a thread.

I wanted to be more and feel better, and at moments I did, but then the overwhelming sadness showed up eventually. I began to take note of what I was eating at first and thought: *Well, that sugar overload isn't helping; that's a culprit!* It was for sure, but even when I adjusted it, Sadness came back knocking. I noticed what I was watching on TV. I had chosen to long forgo the endless breaking news of Covid-19 and political drama, so that wasn't the culprit. But suddenly, while driving in my car, I noticed my playlist that originally was set to play songs like one of my favorite artists, John Mayer, was an endless melody of love, romance, heart break flooding my car, and furthermore, my drowning newly divorced lonely soul! Aha, time to change the channel. That was something my ex-husband used to say regarding playing the broken record in my mind. Nowadays, it's a playlist that infiltrates our heads.

"For every season, there is a time; a time to mourn, a time to cry, laugh, and rejoice." This was a mourning season, a grieving of the loss of my marriage, my high school sweetheart, my family as I knew it, a loss of my own identity as I knew it. For those who take their spouse's name, you have to decide what you want your name to be! If you don't call that an identity crisis, then I sure don't know what you call one! Anyhow, that alarm bell of the music causing my mood to sink deeper was a wake-up call. Girl, time to get up now, but on some happy tunes and shift the atmosphere. Move to the music. You get to decide when you want to mourn and how long that is for each person, depends. Now in this season of mourning, the enemy wants to leave you there. He wants to isolate and destroy you. Don't let him win. Get up and put your dancing shoes on. Shake the dust off your feet and move on. Move on forward! We are going to the other side.

Day 6

What's your favorite style of dance? How does moving your body freely make you feel?

_____
_____
_____
_____
_____
_____
_____
_____
_____
_____
_____
_____
_____
_____

Gift of Gratitude. What are you grateful for?

_____
_____
_____
_____
_____
_____
_____
_____
_____
_____
_____
_____
_____
_____

Pray

Daily Dose

"Therefore, I tell you, whatever you ask for in prayer, believe that you have received it, and it will be yours."

Mark 11:24 (NIV)

Pray. We think we know how to pray. The word of God clearly tells us how to do this in many scriptures. Why does talking to God seem like we need instructions? Well, we fall easily to distraction, tiredness, and many other challenges that lead us to simply skip it, or it becomes a mundane "bless this food" before we eat, which I admit, I rarely do. I've asked myself why I forget this...well, it's because of a couple reasons. For one, I think every meal is expected, and therefore, I'm simply not all that grateful when I do sit down to eat. Now, let me tell you. If you fast and then you finally get to eat, you will feel thankful then. You will be ready to bless the Lord before devouring that long awaited meal. Your taste buds will now dance with excitement to basic and familiar flavors that were just so humdrum before.

So, it is with prayer. When our life is settled or there's not a catastrophe grabbing our emotional heart strings, we tend to do the mundane basic prayer. However, if a fearful moment with a loved one takes place, we cry out to God. I'm certainly not shaming anyone from only praying when we "feel in need." We should go to God then. However, when going through an emotional catastrophe like divorce, I learned to pray even better with hunger, not only a hunger for God to heal my heart and meet financial and mental needs just to make it through the day, but a hunger for Him to make me better and not bitter.

I've found what is so incredibly awesome about God is that when we begin to talk and begin to listen, we develop a stronger bond. That is the higher gift and reward of prayer. It's not just the seen answers to prayers, but your relationship with God becomes stronger. It's like rebuilding a friendship with someone you love, and you've lost your connection. It feels so good and safe to know your friend still loves you and is always there for you. Yes, they might give you some pointers that you may or not be ready to hear, but moreover, they are with you…no matter what!

When you feel alone and discarded as divorce can often leave you feeling, what God wants most is to revive and rekindle your friendship. He's the greatest love of your life. He always has been and always will be. Be reminded of that when you pray and tell him ALL your heart. I mean all, your hurt, anger, loneliness, rage, malice, fears, doubts and insecurities, and what you feel good about. He knows anyhow but wants to know you can safely share it with Him, and He's the source of your every need.

As a child, I remember watching the show *Bewitched*. Now, I'm not encouraging witchcraft; it is a real thing. In this comic show with actress Barbara Eden, she would touch her nose and wiggle it and voila! She was in a new place; she would transport from her 1950's living room to a sunny beach 3,000 miles away. She would go there to talk to someone, usually her crafty mother who was always up to something.

Prayer is a transportation device. It allows you to immediately leave this space you are in mentally and emotionally and enter heaven. Imagine yourself walking up to the throne and approaching God. Now when you clasp your hands, imagine you are now leaving earth and entering heaven. Whatsoever a man asks, it shall be given. Ask for the help and strength, the wisdom, and all you need. Your Father is waiting to provide it. He's here and on the other side waiting for you.

Day 7

Pray (Praise, Repent, Ask, Yield) daily and often. Talk to God. List your prayer request here and come back later to see what's been answered.

_____
_____
_____
_____
_____
_____
_____
_____
_____
_____
_____
_____
_____
_____
_____

What are you grateful for today?

_____
_____
_____
_____
_____
_____
_____
_____
_____
_____
_____
_____

Grieve

Daily Dose

"Blessed is those who mourn, for they will be comforted."

Matthew 5:4 (NIV)

Today with social media pulling at our every moment, we can distract ourselves until we pass out. We don't want to feel pain ever, and I do mean ever. We avoid it like the plague. We constantly scroll looking for more to make us laugh and to connect to others, but often we do it at the cost of real connection to others and ourselves. I urge you today to set aside time to grieve. At the beginning of my separation, I threw myself into work, which at the time was extremely overwhelming. We were coming back full force to work after the adjustment to the pandemic; we had new administration, new software, new staff…new everything. It was a blessing, but mercy was it stressful at the time. Thankfully, I had a supervisor whom I could talk to about what major life changes I was going through, and she afforded me the ability to take some time off.

During this time, I was able to reflect. One day, I laid in my bed and mentally began to process that my marriage after 23 years was over. The tears came, and the gut-wrenching pain of hurt and feeling of being left began to hit me. I did not try to cover it and choke back the tears. It was a full-on ugly cry, groaning mourning. Afterwards, I took a bath, and you know what…. I felt better. "Tears are toxic. They hold toxins, and you need to rid yourself of them. The only way to is through." This is a phrase my sweet therapist often said. Through the valley of pain onward to the hill of hope. Take time to grieve today.

Slow it down; stop it all. Don't avoid this major step towards healing. It may look different for each person, but I promise you, we all need to grieve. You may be grieving the loss of your dreams, your future. It's the loss of not knowing if you will ever be loved or in a relationship again - the loss of your family unit and just simply life as you know it. *A loss is a loss is a loss.* That's the phrase that kept repeating in my mind for some days as I moved through the process of grief. All losses must be grieved. Healing is on the other side of grief, so it's especially important that you truly don't run from it because you prolong your healing by doing so.

    Some people jump into other relationships quickly to avoid this pain. I urge you not to. It is a sneaky cover up of your pain, leading to missed opportunities to get in tune with yourself and your creator. I encourage you to remember that God is here and around the corner.

Day 8

What things do you need to grieve?
How might you express these losses?

_____
_____
_____
_____
_____
_____
_____
_____
_____
_____
_____
_____
_____

Even in grief, there is something to
be thankful for today. List it here:

_____
_____
_____
_____
_____
_____
_____
_____
_____
_____
_____
_____

Serve

Daily Dose

"But seek first his kingdom and his righteousness, and all these things will be given to you as well."

Matthew 6:33 (NIV)

Let's talk about serving. During my separation, I had committed previously to serving in my church's Christmas play. I love acting and all things theatre. I performed pre-Covid. I loved the whole process, which included being around other creative people, challenging myself to learn lines and being on stage. However, this time around, I felt quite inadequate mentally, emotionally, and physically to keep my commitment. However, I promised it was God first and then myself. Anytime I was tempted to wimp out on this promise, I would say God...You...God...You. Putting myself in second place was a new phenomenon. I had been accustomed to serving others first, but in doing so, I had depleted myself over the years, and I had nothing left to pour from my cup. My kids were older now and needed less of my energy and time, and well, it was just me and God in that house most days. Therefore, I stuck to my promise and how God blessed me in the smack dab middle of my hurricane of emotions.

During rehearsals, it was only then I could focus and stop worrying about my current personal situation. Not only could I focus most days, but I also began thriving there in that creative little heaven. I was laughing and smiling, and I felt joy. It doesn't have to be at church. It could be at work, a community organization, your extended family, or neighbors. Wherever it is, just go serve, and I promise you'll find joy in doing it. You deserve joy today, and God deserves your service.

Day 9

How might you serve God's purpose
in your community?

Gratitude Check In:

Rejoice

Daily Dose

"The LORD has done it this very day;
let us rejoice today and be glad."
Psalm 118:24 (NIV)

"Today's a new day, but there is no sunshine, nothing but clouds, and it's dark in my heart, and it feels like a cold night." Those are the words from Kirk Franklin's song "Smile." I really relate to those lyrics. The word of God says, "His praise will continually be in my mouth." We think: *How can we rejoice when we are so hurt, sad, and broken?* The truth is…perspective. Gratitude is difficult during this time in your life, but it is more important than ever, and I do mean ever. You are wired to give Him praise. He inhabits the praise of His people. So, who is God, and why do I want him to inhabit me? Well, He is all the things you need to survive right now; He is joy, love, forgiveness, kindness, strength, power, all-knowing, and more.

Before you get out of bed, if you can't yet think of three things to be grateful for, I challenge you just to begin by saying, "Thank You Lord." You may not feel like it, but I guarantee it will activate the literal neurons in your brain to feel better, and if you really want to feel better, say it again and again. Whether it's a warm bed, life, your kids, your job, your food, your health, your parents, your clothes, your hair, your eyes, and whatever you can muster, just try. You are worth it; you are worthy, but moreover, He is worthy.

Day 10

Smile!
What else can you rejoice about this week?

_____

Who will you tell them you're grateful for them in your life? List them and then call or text them to tell them why.

_____

Roadblocks and Detours

Daily Dose

"I will go before you and will level the mountains; I will break down gates of bronze and cut through bars of iron."
Isaiah 45:2 (NIV)

So...here's the thing about going to the other side, there will be massive roadblocks and unexpected detours. Simply count on them, so when they occur, you can relax and just say, "Oh yeah, Felisha warned me about this." There are blessings ahead, and the enemy also knows it. The enemy can't stop God and His blessings, so he's going to try to delay you. The enemy will use things (roadblocks/detours), such as anger, depression, and bitterness, to get you stuck, tempting you to give up.

On my journey to the other side, one of my gauges had malfunctioned and wasn't working properly. This gauge we will call trust. My trust gauge had been damaged not only by others but myself. Could I trust myself to look out for myself after letting my guard down and being left and hurt after 23 years of marriage to someone I trusted since I was a child? Understandably so, that trust gauge was out of whack. One week was overwhelmingly challenging for me. My mind had a lot of difficulty processing. I wasn't quite sure if I was still reeling from the emotional and mental trauma of the divorce or if it was my new migraine medicines. Perhaps it was the mini concussion that I suffered in my car wreck. We will save that discussion for another day! All I knew for sure was that I was having extreme difficulty making decisions.

At first, it was deciding on my son's graduation photos, and then I began to think that it was difficult because I was also letting him go in the process. Next, it was big projects that I couldn't decide upon like writing this book or another one, then work projects, then who I should and should not let in my life, then simple stuff like what nail polish I should wear. My trust meter had been damaged not only by others but myself. Could I trust myself to look out for myself after letting my guard down and being left and hurt after 23 years of marriage to someone I trusted since I was a child?

Nothing can damage your trust gauge more than divorce. It will expose the worst in those you love and sometimes the worst in yourself. What I saw in me was fear, lack of boundaries, and inability to take care of myself and see my worth. Let me tell you that your worth is not in being a wife, a mother, or any other title or accolade. It's not in your beauty, size, or intelligence. It simply isn't, and don't let petty folks, no matter if they are best friends or your momma, tell you otherwise. I'm here to tear down society and the devil's lies. Your worth is how God sees you! You are to die for. You have gifts, and He made you fearfully and wonderfully, whether you are bean-pole skinny or round and bouncy. Look within and look to Him to define you and build your trust in Him; then trust in yourself, and trusting others will flow from it.

Day 11

What are some emotional roadblocks
you have run into?
What detours did you find yourself taking?
Ask God to help you with these.

_____
_____
_____
_____
_____
_____
_____
_____
_____
_____
_____
_____

Today I'm grateful for:

_____
_____
_____
_____
_____
_____
_____
_____
_____
_____
_____
_____

Angry Avenue

Daily Dose

*"In your anger do not sin:
Do not let the sun go down while you are still angry."*

Ephesians 4:26 (NIV)

This is one of your first stops on the detour. I recall feeling angry at not only being in this situation of divorce after so many years of commitment but also angry at myself for trusting. It quickly spilled over to others. That's the thing about anger; it's like a red-eyed villain. I loved watching *X-men* as a child, and I went to every movie and followed the story into my adulthood. I recall one episode where the X-men, Gene Gray, became angry, and her eyes turned a burning red, and she wasn't able to control it. Soon, she was wreaking havoc on everyone, even those she loved. Her piercing red eyes laser cut through anyone she looked upon and eventually killed those closest to her. That's the thing about anger; it's hard to control. While it's understandable, the pain results in anger, so you must go to God to ask Him to help you manage it properly. Otherwise, you might find yourself snapping on family, friends and coworkers. It may be the slightest thing to set you off, and when you are already emotionally depleted, next thing you know you're the good guy turned villain.

The saying "hurt people hurt people" is very true. Here's the thing few people say, "We're all hurting in some way." I think the deeper thought should be identifying your hurt and working to heal it properly. If so, then you are less likely to wreak Gene Gray havoc! When she became fully aware of her pain and the source of it and dealt with it properly, she could then cease destroying everyone around her.

Day 12

What things have made you feel angry?
Talk to God about your feelings and ask Him to help you deal properly.

_____
_____
_____
_____
_____
_____
_____
_____
_____
_____
_____
_____
_____
_____

I can still find things to be grateful for like:

_____
_____
_____
_____
_____
_____
_____
_____
_____
_____

Curve of Confidence

Daily Dose

"I praise you because I am fearfully and wonderfully made; your works are wonderful; I know that full well."
Psalm 139:14 (NIV)

You might find that your confidence takes an unexpected curve. You may feel yourself swerving off the straight-ahead road of feeling surprisingly good about yourself to one that suddenly plummets into a ditch. The good thing is that there will be warning signs that let you know the curve is coming and you need to adjust and hold on tight to the wheel. There's the sign of comparison; it ranges from a muted subtle green to fluorescent. There you might be scrolling on social media, and you see your ex showing off his new love interest, or they are simply smiling and looking as though they are loving life! Then if you dare to look at their comments, other random strangers are giving them hearts and likes, and goodness forbid red hot flames...this is where the sign turns florescent. If you're wise, you click off the app or find a cute puppy or cat feed to calm your nerves. However, the damage has been done, and your confidence has already been hit as well.

Other moments, such as depression, weight gain, weight loss, and not having energy to spruce yourself up, can also hit your confidence hard. You miss hearing the compliments however authentic or inauthentic they may have been that you were conditioned to get from your former spouse, every now and then. Perhaps it's none of that, and there's just this void of another person being around. You could also be experiencing financial hardships, and that too has impacted your confidence in the ability to provide and take care of yourself, your children, and others dependent on you.

I got it all. I felt it all. I was so low sometimes I could not wait to get home and get in my bed, and I wished I could stay there and cry, or at my worst, I wished I wasn't there at all. There are moments when you need to grieve, cry, and pull the covers over your head and shut out the world. I give you permission. What you don't want to do is stay there. We are going to the other side. This is just a curve, so hang on tight to the wheel, slow down, and if you dare, while you are there, stick your head out the window and shout if you need. We are going to the other side.

Day 13

Write down any ways that your confidence has been shaken. Ask God to remind you how special you are and how to build your confidence.
You are His favorite child.

_____

I'm grateful to have these qualities:

Detour to Depression

Daily Dose

*"So do not fear, for I am with you;
do not be dismayed, for I am your God.
I will strengthen you and help you;
I will uphold you with my righteous right hand."*
Isaiah 41:10 (NIV)

So...I got stuck on a detour. This road to depression can sneak up on you. You'll be traveling alone along this new road of divorce, and suddenly the road ahead is closed, and now you find yourself on this winding detour. Like all detours, you don't plan for it, not really, but there it is, a sudden reroute of your intended destination. I want to let you know you can still and will come out on the other side, but you must recognize this is a detour - a Depression Tour. It's not very scenic; in fact, it's often dark, unpaved, and bumpy roads that may find you in tears. And just like any time you must change paths, like Google maps, it will instantly recalculate your ETA (estimated time of arrival). Now, you have been rerouted; it is going to take longer to get where you are going, but if you stay focused on the destination, you will still get there. Now along this road, you must be careful because there are sharp curves and catastrophic cliffs that can even lead to thoughts of suicide or just wishing you were gone, nonexistent. I like to also think if you find yourself here on this detour that it's just the valley before the incline on the way to the mountain.

Recently, I've been so fortunate to hear a plethora of guest speakers who have mentioned what their low valley felt like. One such renowned author, Rick Rigsby, said after the sudden death of his wife early in their marriage, his heart didn't beat for two years. That may be how you feel right now, as if you're dead and verily physically alive. We all want love, and when divorce ceases that flow of what we think or believe to be love or even is love, we can find ourselves left feeling as if what is the point of life. I'm here to tell you there is a point, and what you have experienced as my pastor has said "is God-filtered." Then if this catastrophic event has been allowed by our all-knowing and loving Father, who wants and has good gifts for us, then we must be in pursuit of looking for the "good" from this evil hurt.

    The author I mentioned above, well, his story didn't stop there. He went on to say after those two years, suddenly his heart did beat again, and he found more love when he met his second wife. Even if you don't find a second love, God knows, and I promise you, He sees your heart and your heart's desire. Trust His heart when you can't trace His hand. I've heard this phrase a lot and wondered about it, so I asked God to help me really understand this and how to do it. I'll come back, and let you know what He reveals to me.

Day 14

You are not stuck;
Everything is temporary.

_____
_____
_____
_____
_____
_____
_____
_____
_____
_____
_____
_____

Gratitude will lift you up.
Give yourself this most beautiful gift today.
Name 5 things you are grateful for:

_____
_____
_____
_____
_____
_____
_____
_____
_____

Roadblock...Bitterness

Daily Dose

"Get rid of all bitterness, rage and anger, brawling and slander, along with every form of malice."
Ephesians 4:31 (NIV)

On your way to the other side, you may come across a stretch of highway that is under construction. Here is where you will often find a roadblock. The road isn't closed, but forward motion has been brought to a halt, and we must rethink our direction. Bitterness is a roadblock. The entry sign says 'Welcome All Those Hurting' with a tiny sign, and underneath that continues with the following "Enter here to be sure never to get hurt again, never ever! Do NOT trust anyone!"

Bitterness is a place that no one wants to sojourn for too long, or you will find yourself trapped by anger, vengeance, spite, and even hatred. It's a stench that begins to ooze from your heart if you stay here. Now, it's 100% understandable how you get here... one four letter word: HURT. This HURT is huge and wide, and it's often what's left over from betrayal, abandonment, confusion, and grief. The hurt extends beyond your former spouse, often to include friends, family, children, and their sometimes unintentionally lack of understanding and sometimes simply unwise and unaware council that diminishes your pain or throws a dart of judgment your way. I had my feelings of ALL these emotions and experiences and the hurt can tailspin me into depression and eventually, even rage!

This is a normal roadblock on the way to The Other Side. I began to camp out here after I had no one, but after many occasions with friends and family that they, let's say, missed the mark on wise counsel. Wisdom comes from the Lord, but unfortunately people use common phrases like "just get over it" and "quit your crying" and call it wisdom. You even tell yourself about these things at times. Ignorance gets passed from generation to generation until someone tests the status quo with tools like therapy and self-compassion, and then they come out on the other side. Let that someone be you - setting future generations free with the knowledge of how to embrace and examine your feelings, own them, and invite God into them. Yes, He's a God who cares how you feel, you think, and you live. Let prayer meet the practical. He wants to be in your heart, mind, body, and soul so you can live life abundantly. God is LOVE; there is no greater emotion than that.

Day 15

List any signs of bitterness that is coming up in your life. Ask Holy Spirit to help cut it off at the root.

_____
_____
_____
_____
_____
_____
_____
_____
_____
_____
_____
_____
_____
_____

Gratitude helps heal bitterness.
What are you grateful for today?

_____
_____
_____
_____
_____
_____
_____
_____
_____
_____
_____

Dead End Street

Daily Dose

"I will not die but live and will proclaim what the LORD has done."

Psalm 118: 17 (NIV)

There may be a very deadly street you come across... Suicide Street. Do not go down this path. The enemy may temp you to give up with whispers like "no one cares about you... anyway...why do you keep going? Give up; give in." Don't...just don't. Better days are coming. I promise. We are still yet going to the other side. I know because I came across this street on my journey to the other side, and I know others who will tell you they did as well. It's a very lonely and dark, secluded place. Most won't admit to having been here. Why? It's a place where egos die; that's for sure. No ego ever survived wandering down suicide street. Now, egos aren't from God, but confidence is. My son has a tattoo that has the lyrics from a gospel song. It says, "I will rest in your promises."

My confidence is your faithfulness." He's faithful, even when we don't feel or see it. Say the Together prayer with me holding your hands and these very words... "Together Lord, I will rest in your promises; my confidence is in Your faithfulness." Say it repeatedly until it gets down deep in your spirit, cry it, plead it, and rest, truly rest in it. You don't have to do anything but trust Him and rest knowing He will take care of you. I love you and so does He. Keep going; tomorrow will be better; the next minute will be better; the next second will be better; just keep going. I'm with you; He's with you, and we are all going to the other side. Here we go now, one step forward...together.

Day 16

What do you look forward to in the future?
Think about these things.

_____
_____
_____
_____
_____
_____
_____
_____
_____
_____
_____
_____

**If you are feeling particularly low, you can talk to God and people who serve as His earthly angels.
There is immediate help: National Suicide Prevention line: Dial 988 or
1-800-273-TALK(8255)**

Today be reminded that you are grateful to be alive! What are 3 things you can feel grateful for in this moment?

_____
_____
_____
_____
_____
_____
_____

Stuck in Traffic

Daily Dose

*"He lifted me out of the slimy pit, out of the mud and mire;
he set my feet on a rock and gave me a firm place to stand."*

Psalm 40:2 (NIV)

Have you ever gotten stuck in the mud? Oh boy, I have. Your wheels just keep spinning and spinning, digging yourself deeper and deeper into the ground with each time you turn the engine over. You can feel the car rocking and sinking, and you eventually give up and must step outside. When you know good well, it's going to mess up your shoes, so you better hope you wore something a bit less cute that day or at a minimum, washable.

I once had a little 86' Blue Corolla that I had nicknamed Bluebell. Now, Bluebell was my second car after I had totaled my first one. She was sweet but not always nice at long traffic lights. She would purr like a kitten, and then suddenly you'd find her snoring like Garfield if the light was red a bit too long. That's when it would happen; she'd be off to her little cat nap. Of course, that's the exact time the light would turn green, and suddenly I'd have to jump out, thrust my shoulder into the cab with one hand on the steering wheel, and lean into it as I push with my legs and get her either out of the way or back into motion and on our way. Thankfully, my stocky, strong legs came in very handy in those moments where I otherwise found great displeasure in them. They graced me in these moments, and I thanked them for their power.

God graces us for moments when we get stuck. He has truly equipped us in ways we can't imagine.

As a young girl, all of 5'3 and 125, I was in no way intimated to move an entire car immediately. I had grown up on a farm with two brothers and knew how to fend for myself quite well as a true country girl. No panic set in for me during this moment of being stuck with oncoming traffic, horns honking and such. I just simply used what God gave me and went into action. Some days you might get emotionally stuck. I've been there, too. You might find yourself spinning and going over scenarios, hurtful moments and what-ifs and oh-ifs. This ...then. This. The enemy is great at slinging mud and trying to drag you under but remember the power God has given you. Step out, put your shoulder into it, dig deep, and push forward. We are going to the other side.

Day 16

What are some of gifts God has given you to help you fight back when you feel stuck?

_____
_____
_____
_____
_____
_____
_____
_____
_____
_____
_____
_____
_____

Recall a time when you were grateful to get unstuck. Write it here.

_____
_____
_____
_____
_____
_____
_____
_____
_____
_____
_____
_____
_____

Missteps, Stumbles and All Out Tumbles (Rocky Road)

Daily Dose

"And the God of all grace, who called you to his eternal glory in Christ, after you have suffered a little while, will himself restore you and make you strong, firm and steadfast."

1 Peter 5:10 (NIV)

Oh boy, we just turned onto a rocky road, and I'm not talking about that Ben & Jerry's Ice-cream flavor, nothing tasty here. Oh, there will be lots of falls, I'd say. You'll get tripped up on this journey; otherwise, you are simply not going anywhere. Let me confide in you, my blunder. Unfortunately, this is going to be embarrassing, but it is also going to show how brave I am, and in that I take courage in telling you. So here goes…I got catfished. Yes, me the Christian lady not looking for a relationship, but looking for God to bring me hope of a friend and perhaps one day someone who might find me worthy of love. Here's how it happened. I ran into a coworker in the lady's restroom. She told me of a famous actress who had prayed a specific prayer for a husband and asked God what she wanted. Therefore, I in act of vulnerability and faith whispered a little prayer to God that perhaps I wasn't done with love and that there would be an ideal mate out there, even at the age of 47 after feeling discarded by my childhood sweetheart that I thought to be "the one," which apparently wasn't "the one." I had so much unbridled anger against him for how things ended; he was the last "one" I wanted to be "the one." Clearly, I had been wrong for all 23 years and got it wrong, and the blessing was my boys, but I wanted a right mate, a good fit, a partner to do life with…to get up in the morning with, to eat breakfast with, dinner with, enjoy life with…truly partner with…not wonder when they are coming home and home be the loneliest place there was…for so many years. It most certainly was just that! Give me more God! Please give me what you want God and a man after your own heart! I was putting my prayers out there into the stratosphere and into His hands, right… well, it so happens a mirror conversation happens with another one of my friend's moms later that same day.

By mirror conversation, I mean it was almost a duplicate message…"Felisha, you know God knows the desires of your heart, right, don't you?" she said in this most reassuring motherly voice…
"Right? Don't you? He knows…"
I responded, "Yea, I know in a feeble, oh yea of little faith tone."

And there she goes on to tell me about this same actress…and her struggles…what on earth? Is this Viola Davis Day? Meanwhile, I go about my day and after checking my social media I noticed an attractive looking fellow requesting to follow me…Should I…follow back? Respond back? Maybe, I'm scared, ah, what the heck…here goes nothing... Click! And there I was out into the world, talking with a stranger. Was it fate, an answered prayer all in same day? Maybe, just maybe…and so I proceed with caution. And I do mean caution, like yellow light blinking, holding stop signs while tip toeing with a caution vest on….I'm literally telling him every time he text something nice …that's a red flag…and another red flag…but at the same time…I keep showing up as he's showing up and testing it out day by day …and just when it seems like this handsome Christian guy is legit, he asks for $200 to keep his internet in Iraq! Really, stop the presses… what just happened…close up the shop! Who is this? A 19-year-old in Africa, Botswana, down the street? Who knows? I've been scammed or at least attempted to be! I'm out! I'm glad I'm only in a week; however, I was incredibly angry with myself for letting my guard down, and then I thought, *you know, it was fun while it lasted and you know it does go to show that I have potential to love again, to be open again.* I need to be selective, but I'm not dead. There is perhaps…love out there…and maybe it's just a click away on the other side.

Day 17

How might you be vulnerable with God and write down the desires of your heart here? May you trust Him with all your heart.

_____
_____
_____
_____
_____
_____
_____
_____
_____
_____
_____
_____

I am grateful for:

_____
_____
_____
_____
_____
_____
_____
_____
_____
_____
_____

Why You Are

Daily Dosage

*"Your eyes saw my unformed body;
all the days ordained for me were written in your book
before one of them came to be."*

Psalm 139:16 (NIV)

These are beautiful affirmations.
I suggest you speak them over yourself daily:
God is the great I am!
I am His creation.
I am fearfully and wonderfully made;
I am a child of God.
I am the head and not the tail.

Now we know who you are. Do you know WHY you are?

These prophetic thoughts and ponderings don't come from me. They come from God. During my typical morning routine of watching sermons via YouTube, God led me to an offbeat music video of a group of unique and quirky artists strumming guitars and beating drums in a tiny bedroom making their own melodramatic melody. The lead singer pauses between one song and says, "Well, we know who you are, but it's the why you are... we are still trying to figure that out." In that moment, I thought *ok, God, that's why you led me here to this video.* So it is throughout your life, good and bad moments, look around and take note and see and find and if you cannot find ... ask... Is this why I'm here God? For this; for them?

He has so many special moments for us to share, enjoy, grow, learn, smile, feel, and do for others.... all things. Life can get busy and filled up with who we are: our title, our goals, and identity even negative associated ones like divorced ... and we miss the Why we are. Don't you dare give up! Why you are here is far reaching, and God has big plans for you to enjoy, and others need your help and gift to make it. We are going to the other side; that is why you are reading this today. Be reminded of WHY you are today.

List 3 Affirmations.
List three reasons Why you are here:

_____
_____
_____
_____
_____
_____
_____
_____
_____
_____
_____
_____

Be grateful for yourself today.
Here's what I'm grateful to myself for:

_____
_____
_____
_____
_____
_____
_____
_____
_____
_____
_____
_____

Shifting Gears

Daily Dose

"I will purge you of those who revolt and rebel against me. Although I will bring them out of the land where they are living, yet they will not enter the land of Israel. Then you will know that I am the LORD."

Ezekiel 20:38 (NIV)

I heard an immensely powerful message today by Stephen Furtick. Is it threshing or attack? God may be very well cutting away something negative from your life that diminishes your life to reserve the kernel. A kernel is particularly important. Things grow from the kernel. However, the husk must be pulled away. I recall shucking corn as a child; a whole wagon full! It was a lot of work, but I loved it when my mom boiled that corn, and I salted and buttered it. I would hold it and run my teeth over it and eat it as if it were a typewriter, and at the end of each row, I mentally did a cha-ching in my head all the while unconsciously humming like a motor.

I shamingly admit I still find myself doing it as an adult when food is really good to me...I hum. Once while eating, one of my friends said, "Wait! What's that noise?" So, I stopped eating to listen, and I did not hear a thing. "What noise?" I replied.

"It stopped," she responded. Afterward, I would go back to eating, and she said, "There it is again..." At that moment, it occurred to her: "It's you! You are the humming sound!" She and I had a good hardy laugh until we almost cried. No matter how hard

I tried to stop my humming, it would eventually return because the food was just that good to me!

The work of getting to the good part is a process, and it's often laborious, hard, and tiring. You may be ready to quit in the process, but when it's finally prepared, all that work seems worth it after that first bite. So, it is in the pulling away from your spouse. The process is painful and laborious, and I was so sure it was the devil, but just what if it's God shucking the corn and getting you ready to prepare you for a more enjoyable life full of flavor and salt? Every day you might be humming inside from pleasure of its taste. That idea makes it not hurt so bad.

Day 18

What type of issues, individuals, or attitudes might God be purging from your life?

_____
_____
_____
_____
_____
_____
_____
_____
_____
_____
_____
_____
_____

I am grateful for these changes happening in my life:

_____
_____
_____
_____
_____
_____
_____
_____
_____
_____
_____
_____
_____
_____

Not All It's Yoked Up to Be

Daily Dose

"Do not be yoked together with unbelievers. For what do righteousness and wickedness have in common? Or what fellowship can light have with darkness?"

2 Corinthians 6:14 (NIV)

I've always heard the phrase "unequally yoked." We quote the scripture, but do we really understand it? I didn't. Therefore, I looked up the meaning in the dictionary. That's what I always do when I really want to drill down and understand something. Ever since I was a child, I loved the dictionary, and one dorky nerdy thing I liked to do was read it. It's about the only nerdy thing I liked as a child, but those set of Britannica encyclopedias my parents bought were quite valuable ... this was pre-internet dial up, of course.

Here's what Google said: a *yoke* is a control device used to tie two animals together to reap the full benefits of plowing and carrying a burden. Now, when two alike animals, a cow and another cow, are yoked, they move at the same pace, but when a donkey and a cow are yoked, it makes for a difficult job, and you cannot get much done.

I recall when we sat our children down to tell them about the divorce. My husband said cheerfully, "Mom likes to go slow, and I like to go fast." I remained quiet but thought inside: *what a sap sorry way for him to try to justify him just wanting to do whatever he wants and leave his commitments*, but you know I stayed quiet to support my kids and just to keep the peace in this moment.

Later, I thought that it was true. I thought we were never supposed to be together; then, the thought followed that our kids are gifts of God, and they are a blessing. It was for a season; then, the counter acting thought came... *what God has joined together, let no man put asunder.*

I was trying so hard to make sense of the ending by examining the beginning. However, you have to review all parts in between and evaluate it with God's word. I will go back to this unequally yoked specific instructions ... He says, "do not be with unbelievers!" Why? God is not guiding them, and they are going to lead you astray; you'll fight on fundamental beliefs, and that had begun to happen. His beliefs shifted away from God as mine shifted more towards God. Now, this is not to throw shade but rather to cast light. The truth always casts light. Ask God to show you where you might have been unequally yoked, so you can come to the acceptance of His truth. When you find that truth, you can grow from it and have more peace. It does not make the hurt go away, but it does silence some confusion and condemnation. There is no condemnation in those who love the Lord, Christ Jesus. "Take my yoke upon you for it is easy and light."

Day 19

List any areas you may have become unequally yoked.
Ask God to reveal any way that did not please Him.

_____
_____
_____
_____
_____
_____
_____
_____
_____
_____
_____
_____

Gratitude in action.
Who will you express gratitude to today?

_____
_____
_____
_____
_____
_____
_____
_____
_____
_____
_____
_____

Letting Go, Letting Go

Daily Dose

"Then Esau said, 'Let us be on our way; I'll accompany you.'"

Genesis 33:12 (NIV)

It was a fight that ended all fights. I had it with ignoring me, chewing me out, and arguing until the wee hours of morning, coming home to an empty garage, and just being married to someone who did not want to be married as he had told me several times before. He asked me the question that he had so many times before, and I said no, but he wanted a yes: "So, you want a divorce?" It was a cajoling question; like come on, just say yes…so I did in that moment. He was relieved because he had been pretending to want to be there and not such a good job of pretending by the clear absence of his presence in our home or coming home often 2-3 hours later than what he had said. I recall the arguments, not wanting to take me to the doctor and the blatant disregard of my presence and ignoring me to pour himself into that handheld device that had become part of his hand. It was over before it was over. When I relented the next morning, he became even angrier and gave me a resounding, "no!" Therefore, I immediately said, "I release you then; I release you."

Months later listening to my Calm app, which I tell you is divine healing within it…the narrator said these words…letting go, letting go, letting…go. It was so soothing in her subtle, kind, and gentle voice as she was explaining how to be released from all things. There comes a time when you must let go. Let go of negativity, let go of people who do not want to stay, and let go of your plans. It can hurt deeply to let go; that is the beginning of grieving. However, on the other side, there is peace in knowing you are with people who want to be with you, peace in knowing you are in control of your emotions about the changes that are happening, and peace in knowing you cannot do it all, and you were not meant to. Let go and let God.

Day 20

What things are you struggling to let go?
How might letting go benefit you?

_____
_____
_____
_____
_____
_____
_____
_____
_____
_____
_____
_____

I am grateful to be able to let go of these things:

_____
_____
_____
_____
_____
_____
_____
_____
_____
_____
_____
_____
_____

Bad Directions

Daily Dose

*"There is a way that appears to be right,
but in the end it leads to death."
Proverbs 14:12 (NIV)*

Oops! We just missed our exit! Looks like we have got to keep going and get off on the next one and loop back around. We've all experienced the frustration of a wrong turn or a missed exit. Sometimes it gets us way off course from our destination and planned arrival time, but eventually we find our way. Many years ago, I recall driving my oldest son to his football game, and this was in the days before everyone's phone had GPS. In fact, only the most travelled folks had the fancy Garmin GPS devices that you installed and hung from your windshield. Like mostly everyone else, we took the internet and printed, yes, printed out a hard copy of directions from MapQuest. The drive was approximately an hour away, and I gave myself ample time to get there, but what I did not plan on was there being two roads with the same name in two different opposite directions. This did not occur to me until we were way out in the boondocks when I stopped at a gas station to get verbal directions, and the attendant told me such nonsense! I was livid at MapQuest but relieved to get back on track. At this point, we were pushing being late to the game, but supermom turned Mario Andretti kicked into gear. We rushed back onto the interstate headed back in the direction we came, and as I began to merge into the road, another car did not want to let me. That's it! I shook my fist at him in anger! "You're letting me in!" I yelled. "I am getting my boy to his game!!!"

My son said, "Mom, calm down! It is okay!" Thank God for his voice of reason. He was right. I calmed down and accepted we were going to be late and better late and arrive safely. I also immediately decided to order a fancy Garmin, too, to avoid such bad directions in the future. In marriage and relationships, you get all kinds of bad directions or advice. Sure enough, it will land you in a place you do not intend lost, frustrated, and asking anyone nearby for correct ones to get you back on track. The good thing is wrong turning leads to learning. You learn short cuts; you learn sometimes there are no shortcuts. You learn to sit in traffic and wait it out, and yes, you learn that even if you veer off, you will get back on track. The Bible and Holy Spirit are God's gifts to us to give us extremely specific instructions to get on track and get to your destination safely. I urge you to upgrade to those spiritual GPS tools to get you and keep you on track.

Day 21

Is there in any way you may have made a wrong turn and you need to turn around to get back on track? List some times or moments that come to mind and how you can get back on track guided by God's word.

_____
_____
_____
_____
_____
_____
_____
_____
_____
_____
_____
_____
_____
_____

I am grateful for these changes happening in my life:

_____
_____
_____
_____
_____
_____
_____
_____
_____
_____
_____

Life Support

Daily Dose

*"One who has unreliable friends soon comes to ruin,
but there is a friend who sticks closer than a brother."*

Proverbs 18:24 (NIV)

    I could literally write an entire book on this one topic. My friends and family were my life support. I literally would have died had it not been for them propping me up, praying for me, encouraging me, and being beside me daily, monthly, every minute, and every second, even in the pushing away and the ever so needy moments of my pain and hurt that were deep and wide. They were there, and there were many. There were calls, texts, sermon texts, dinners, lunches, and everything in between. God sent me old ones and new ones, and just when I thought I had worn them out, here came some more, and the old ones came back around again. Good Lord, He is good, and He gave me a band of brothers and sisters---my momma, my brothers, my daddy, cousins, friends who are truly sisters, coworkers who became extra brothers and nephews. It was astonishing. New members at my church in Divorce Care had astonishingly similar pains and burdens to bear with me, and we could lift each other up. There were moms whose sons played basketball with mine, and we adopted the term the Mom Coalition! They, too, lifted me up and had no idea how hard it was to go sit at a game and be alone to a man I had been married for 23 years and instantly felt like complete strangers to my estranged spouse. The noticeable separation was on display for the entire gym to witness. I worried my son felt the embarrassment on the court. His teammates rallied around him like extra brothers; their moms became sisters to me, and I did not have to be alone. My brother and his wife came; friends and family joined in sitting in with me in the stands at games. I tell you I was not breathing on my own; they were my life support.

Don't go on this journey alone. Look to connect. Make the right connections, and they will breathe life into you. I cannot thank them enough.

Day 22

Who are your trusted friends you can lean on?
To whom can you be a friend?

_____
_____
_____
_____
_____
_____
_____
_____
_____
_____
_____
_____

I'm so grateful for these friends and family members:

_____
_____
_____
_____
_____
_____
_____
_____
_____
_____
_____
_____

Transformation (Car Wash)

Daily Dose

"Do not conform to the pattern of this world, but be transformed by the renewing of your mind. Then you will be able to test and approve what God's will is—his good, pleasing and perfect will."

Romans 12:2 (NIV)

    I picked a word for the year, and it was Transformation. Now everyone in his/her mind begins to think, *oh, it's time to drop that 20, 30, 40 plus pounds and get skinny fine, so I can start over with a new partner.* I believed no one wants me at this weight, and besides I don't feel attractive or even worthy unless I "fit in." Let me tell you that you aren't supposed to "fit in". You were made to STAND OUT! Therefore, get fit not to fit in but find joy in moving and be healthy to love yourself beyond what you think is required to love yourself by societal standards. Also, a healthy body aids in a healthy mind. I've had so many wonderful women come alongside me and be a good, kind soul to me.
    One such lady is a friend whose name is also Felicia. Both our sons played ball together, and she befriended me in my darkest hours. I recall the Sunday after we told our boys we were divorcing, and I felt led to go down to the alter and pray at church. I was adamant that we would attend church as a family that day, and so we all went. I told my then husband that I wanted us to go to the altar. The look on his face told me he was reluctant, but nonetheless he did it. I really wanted to provide all the Godly leadership we could for our boys especially and seek prayer during the most difficult time that was ahead of us. In doing so, our son's coach and his wife were waiting at the altar that day, and so we approached them and told them we were getting a divorce. She and

I looked at each other, and immediately she teared up. She could see the pain in my eyes as well. We embraced and prayed as two families.

Later that day, they both text me and my husband offering to counsel us. My husband quickly replied, "No thanks, the decision is final for now." It again reinjured my soul as I had tried many times to rescue the dying relationship, and I felt again, the clear rejection being shown to me in front of others.

I responded, "Thank you, we appreciate your concerns and prayers for us," as I knew it was a closed door that I had been trying to walk through and I could no longer do it by myself. Forward into the basketball season, this dear friend once again showed up for me and left a gym membership in my mailbox. She then became my gym buddy for a time. You don't have to know how things will work out, just know they will. There are angels God is sending to help you get to the other side to transform your life.

Day 23

What is something you want to transform?
Ask God to direct you how to clean it up (whether it's your diet, your busy schedule, etc.)

I am grateful for:

Service Check

Daily Dose

"Each of you should use whatever gift you have received to serve others, as faithful stewards of God's grace in its various forms."

1 Peter 4:10 (NIV)

I love all creative things, obviously, like writing, singing, and acting. I had the wonderful opportunity to act in the Christmas play at my church a few years ago pre-Covid. When the opportunity presented itself again, I was so delighted to jump back in 2021. I even signed up to audition for the dance ensemble in addition to the acting scenes. I was quite thrilled to go to the audition, but I had a frightening occurrence on the way there. A raging motor cyclist rode up beside my vehicle, gave me "the middle finger," and sped off only to find out as I turned into the parking lot of the church, he had followed me approximately 12 miles and then proceeded to chase me through the parking lot. I could not even park without him chasing me down. I was terrified he was going to pull a gun on me. Thankfully, other ladies saw him and walked up to my car as I had 911 on the phone. I reported the incident as they dispatched an officer to ensure everyone's safety.

Sometimes you must push through the hurts, fears, and everything that seems to be holding you back and just serve God anyhow. Serve humanity. Help people. You have two choices: chase service or chase success. By chasing service, it can in return lead to success, but you get to decide the goal. Let me encourage you to be a service chaser.

Day 24

What gifts do you have?
How might you use them to be of service?

_____
_____
_____
_____
_____
_____
_____
_____
_____
_____
_____
_____
_____
_____

What ways are you grateful to be of service?

_____
_____
_____
_____
_____
_____
_____
_____
_____
_____
_____
_____
_____
_____

Filling Your Tank

Daily Dose

*"LORD, you alone are my portion and my cup;
you make my lot secure."*
Psalm 16:5 (NIV)

Today I want you to be reminded to fill your tank or rather your cup. Make your favorite cup or tea or coffee. As you sit and sip on it, stop all distractions and simply sit with it. Hold it in your hands and feel the warmth of the cup. Notice how the heat on your hands is calming and relaxing. Focus on every drop and the flavor it possesses. Don't gulp unless it's just that good. Lol! Try to savor the moment and quiet everything down. Quiet your phone, TV, children's voices, and your inner voices that criticize you constantly. Do not go into a frenzy thinking about what to do next. Just focus on now…there is ONLY now, and each moment to come or before ONLY can be experienced once so soak it in.

"Fill your cup" is a phrase used often in the Bible. The widow, who was not sure how to feed her and her son, was told to go and collect the empty vessels she could find. Can you imagine going around asking people to give you something that you literally didn't have any way of filling it. It's going to take a miracle! I am sure she thought that and never mind how silly she might look to everyone she asked. Well, as we know pride comes before a fall, so thankfully she did not let her pride kill her. It most definitely could have, for she and her child were starving. Well, God showed her that her faith and obedience would be rewarded. He showed her He is there to fill her up, so she could not deny He supplies. His blessings of provision poured out with every vessel that He filled.

Sometimes, we can spend a lot of energy, emotionally and mentally, going through a divorce. We run to lawyers, friends, and family all with our questions, and retell how we are hurt and lacking. They may let you borrow the vessel, which will help you, but only God can fill it. Ask God what you need to do and then ask Him to feel your cup surrounding you with peace, comfort, and warmth just like that delicious drink in your hands. When He does, take a moment to savor His goodness; try not to gulp it down never noticing how good it feels to be filled and then quickly looking for Him to fill it again. He will indeed meet your needs repeatedly but get to know and deeply appreciate Him and His loving nature. He's the best barista I know, and He makes one delicious cup of peace.

Day 25

How did sitting and enjoying your drink make you feel? How can you refill your cup daily to create this joy daily?

_____
_____
_____
_____
_____
_____
_____
_____
_____
_____
_____
_____

What things came to mind that
made you feel grateful?

_____
_____
_____
_____
_____
_____
_____
_____
_____
_____

Filling Other's Tank

Daily Dose
"It is more blessed to give than to receive."
Acts 20:35 (NIV)

It looks as if we have a full tank of gas now that we have been to the gas station to fill up. Our ride looked pretty after coming through the carwash. Now, let us see where we can go. Once your tank has been filled, and you feel renewed, it's a good time to give it to someone else. What God gives to us is often not just for us but for us to then give to others who are in need. Sometimes it is just a gift of encouragement because we feel encouraged. Other times, we may be able to bless others financially because we now have more.

Whatever gift we have been given, we can now regift it. Yes! Regifting of this kind is actually very good. God has called us into reciprocal relationships - ones in which we can pour into each other, emotionally, mentally, and physically by using His loving kindness. Those are the ones you will want to review in your life and maintain a closeness to these individuals. Other times, we may be more on the giving end with some but be careful not to attach so closely to these individuals or you might be left stranded with a very empty tank. That is not to say we leave them stranded either, but you may just be asked to give them a ride down the street - not carry them to the full destination. This is how you break from codependent relationships. You do not stop giving; you just establish how much energy you will put into certain people.

God always finds a way to give back to you what He is asked you to give, but He always wants you to be a good steward as well. I had to learn this concept of pouring out in a new and right way through healing from my divorce. Sometimes it had me agonizing over giving too much or drawing up and closing myself off unable to give freely or allow others to give to me. Holy Spirit showed me how when this is applied well, I am at peace when I give and at peace when I set appropriate boundaries from individuals who drain me. Ok, let us get in this shiny ride, see who needs help, and continue to the other side.

Day 26

Who might you give to today freely without expectation of return? Who in your life is a giver who you can easily help fill one another's tank?

_____
_____
_____
_____
_____
_____
_____
_____
_____
_____
_____
_____

I'm grateful for the opportunity to give from my overflow. List these opportunities here:

_____
_____
_____
_____
_____
_____
_____
_____
_____
_____
_____
_____

Embracing the Quiet

Daily Dosage

"He got up, rebuked the wind and said to the waves, 'Quiet! Be still!' Then the wind died down and it was completely calm."
Mark 4:39 (NIV)

Some people like the quiet; for some, it can be heart wrenching and a reminder of how alone you feel. We often, me included, do not like prolonged quietness. It can feel good at first, but if it goes beyond what is enjoyable, it then can become a thorn of sorrow. It can feel as if you are reminded of feeling disconnected with every second past the comfortable quiet.

I used to look forward to the weekends, but now they hold a bit of gloom around them. I knew there was a whole lot of alone time that no amount of cleaning and tasks could fill. I also felt so empty of energy to get those things done that I needed the weekend to rest, but after waking, there stood the quiet again, staring at me, and looking me in the eye telling me…well, you are still alone. The enemy will come and tell you, "Look at you. You are alone." And why? You are not enough…or your very own mind will review all the most difficult things said to you from the person you believed would always be there, the stuff you cannot even say to anyone else. The stuff that you are still trying to process, just how did they say, do that? And by admitting their actions, you feel the pain and embarrassment of having been in a relationship with them at all, much more felt and believed they loved you and you loved them back for just how many years? The quiet will fill in the gaps on things you do not understand. It may fill in the gaps correctly or incorrectly, but I promise you it will fill them in and then erase the reasons and fill them in again.

    The quiet, quite frankly, can and will make you go crazy in moments. But it is okay…the quiet is part of it all. The quiet will also offer time to reflect, grieve, and find joy in simple things like movies, books, prayer, and a good meal. I recommend you embrace the quiet for these gifts it alone can provide. Start with mediation. I love the app, Calm. It has several guided meditations that help you to navigate and embrace the quiet.

Day 27

How did embracing the quiet make you feel?
What emotions were you able to process?

_____

I am grateful for :

_____

Exploring Your Gifts

Daily Dose
"Therefore, if anyone is in Christ, the new creation has come: The old has gone, the new is here!"
2 Corinthians 5:17 NIV

People might try to tell you don't let this divorce change you. However, I say the exact opposite: It's here to change you. All your experiences have been allowed by God, and this is an opportunity to grow, to change, and to become new and better. Better doesn't look like smiling and skipping through the tulips, either. I'm here to tell you it looks like perhaps, not plugging through and dismissing your emotions, which means there may be a moment, a day, and a week of wallowing as some might call it. I call it sitting in it.

Society and all those who desperately love you do not like dealing with grief, sadness, and depression. No one does. They do have a place though for a moment. You are not meant to camp out there and throw daily pity parties, but to get to the other side, you do have to go through the valley. Again, I said through…not around, over, under, or take a short cut and derail the whole valley. The valley is where you can grow. The valley is low, and I think it's an incredibly wise place to slow down. In doing so, by slowing down your life, you can begin to explore your gifts. You can begin to revisit yourself and stop just filling up others' cups. God quite likely sends the valley to do just these things in your life. If He sent it, you can trust it. In the valley, you will find you have less energy, and energy is very vital to life. Once you are out, well, before you can go on, you have to rest. I never realized this when we entered the pandemic. Everything for a while shut down. You were now required to take stock of your life and see what really matters, what gives you energy rather than just taking it. There was a mass exodus of jobs where people had found themselves "stuck" for years. Sadly, there have also been people waking up to the feeling of "stuck" in bad or toxic relationships that stole energy. It was an opportunity to turn those situations around and pour more into it, so you could get more out. Nevertheless, it was an opportunity to say, "I have given it my all, and I cannot make it work by myself, so I am going to look at myself with what I have left in me and create the best me I can be, the person who God has been calling me to be."

Spend some time on yourself today. Spend time asking God what you should be doing to give you energy and have an abundant life. You are supposed to have an abundant life. I believe the gifts he's given each of us are meant to help give you an abundant life financially, emotionally, and mentally.

Day 28

Find local events that can help you explore your gifts. Write some ways to find your gifts here.

_____
_____
_____
_____
_____
_____
_____
_____
_____
_____
_____
_____

I am grateful for these opportunities to find what gifts I have locked within me.

_____
_____
_____
_____
_____
_____
_____
_____
_____
_____
_____
_____
_____
_____

Reading the Map

Daily Dose

"It is to be with him, and he is to read it all the days of his life so that he may learn to revere the LORD his God and follow carefully all the words of this law and these decrees."
Deuteronomy 17:19 (NIV)

Commit to reading the word of God every day. Nothing changes a life more than the book of life itself; it's your map. Nothing. I don't care what faith you are; begin reading the bible and just see what happens. Open it to test it out. One simple practice I do is listen and read the Bible app daily devotion. It sets the tone for the day. It's literally less than five minutes, but it has the ability to impact the remaining 1435 minutes.

I recommend beginning with the book of John. Begin there and grow from there to read more. It took me months before I got out of the habit of only using my digital Bible. I can tell you there is a difference when you open the book. It is like kneeling when you pray. God appreciates your willingness to forgo comfort and convenience to seek Him. You will also notice you will have to get to know the word more intricately to find books. I had to get used to flipping all over rather than just a quick click. Labor is part of growth. It is like a tiny garden becoming a field.

I recall growing up in the country, and we had fields of corn and peas and all sorts of vegetables. Some I loved - some not so much. Corn was one I was quite fond of; however, the work it took to enjoy was true hard labor to me as a young child. We would get up early and head to the fields and pick until around noon. We would load tons of corn ears on a trailer wagon and tote it back.

Then we would have to spend the rest of the evening shucking and silking that corn to prepare it to eat. It was full grown, golden beaming deliciousness as soon as my mom boiled it and salted and buttered it. I can almost smell it now and taste the salt and butter rolling off each ear. The corn was all the better for all the effort we put in to harvest it.

The word of God is like that. Put some effort in to harvest its wealth of knowledge, and you will find you are all the better for it because you will have a closer relationship to God. How does one build any relationship? Well, only by spending time together and putting in the work...

Day 29

What did you learn from reading today?
How did it impact your day?

_____
_____
_____
_____
_____
_____
_____
_____
_____
_____
_____
_____

Something that I feel grateful about today is:

_____
_____
_____
_____
_____
_____
_____
_____
_____
_____
_____
_____
_____
_____

Tell Your Story

Daily Dose

"If anyone sins because they do not speak up when they hear a public charge to testify regarding something they have seen or learned about, they will be held responsible."
Leviticus 5:1 (NIV)

It is important to tell your story to yourself and select a few trusted friends and your family. Certainly, social media is not the place to blast and post every detail, no matter how painful it is and how much you want to expose your ex. However, I do not believe in holding it all in. Seek out therapy and a few, a very few people, you can share. Why? You need to hear it being told; you need to get it in your spirit what has happened, so you can grow from it. Inasmuch, you are not meant to heal alone.

Humans work best in a community. We are meant to trust others, and as difficult as it can be after a breakup, it is a trick of the enemy to isolate you further. A fortress keeps danger out, but it also lets nothing good in. My Divorce Care teacher left my class with this tidbit of advice upon our last day in it: Trust: start with some in the bank. Yes, it must be earned, but let's just say there's a little in the account when we open our heart to people. Now, they can make more deposits in there or withdraw based upon their actions, but if it is completely empty, you are likely to close the account before you ever give it a chance to accrue interest.

Day 30

What are you holding inside that you need to use your voice to release it? Words are powerful.
Use them for good.

_____
_____
_____
_____
_____
_____
_____
_____
_____
_____
_____
_____

I'm grateful to use my voice to bless these people:

_____
_____
_____
_____
_____
_____
_____
_____
_____
_____
_____
_____

Prepare for Joy

Daily Dose
*"Those who sow with tears
will reap with songs of joy."*
Psalm 126:5 (NIV)

    I want you to prepare for joy. I don't know when it is coming. I just know that it is on the way. Book it like a trip: a planned destination in your future. You won't know your exact arrival date, but that's okay. You can go ahead and think about what you want to do when you get there. Go ahead, dream big. Also, with whom do you want to spend your vacation time? What about the fun outings - fancy dinners or just plain good burgers or tacos you look forward to grabbing? How about outfit planning? Yes, do it!

    I was ever so fortunate to forge a bond with two other lovely ladies through my Divorce Care class. After the class concluded, we decided to keep the friendship going and set up some dinners. It was truly refreshing to encourage each other and just get out of the house to spend some time talking and catching up with each other. We shared some similar experiences, and we could relate to each other without judgement and challenge each other to grow and heal at our own pace. One such time, one of the ladies suggested we do a vision board. We eagerly agreed to the challenge! We took pics and set a date for the time we would to like to have them done and then texted each other our pics. This spurred us all to dream and focus on the next chapters of our lives. Let me tell you: you are worth it! You deserve it! There will come a time along your journey to the other side when you'll begin to think more about your future than your past, and let me tell you, your future looks bright!

Day 31

I dare you to dream! Write them down here and then surrender them to God. Watch miracles happen when you put your hand to the plow.

_____
_____
_____
_____
_____
_____
_____
_____
_____
_____
_____
_____

Gratitude gives you gifts. What are you grateful for?

_____
_____
_____
_____
_____
_____
_____
_____
_____
_____
_____

Unpack Your Heart

Daily Dose
*"Create in me a pure heart, O God,
and renew a steadfast spirit within me."*
Psalm 51:10 (NIV)

I recall having a dream and as soon as I awoke, I knew it was from God. I had arrived with one of my friends at this beautiful hotel. I was scurrying around what seemed like forever with a little red suitcase on wheels. For some odd reason, in my mind, I was restricted to take this small red suitcase into my room. I would get to the door and simply could not go in with the suitcase. Therefore, I just kept strolling around the hallways stressing out, continuously thinking how I would be able to enjoy this wonderful trip, and beautiful hotel if I was not able to take my luggage into my room. Suddenly, it dawned on me, "Aha! I can unpack my suitcase first, put up my necessities." Instantly, I was freed from the mental anguish and only then would my mind allow me to take the suitcase into the room." I felt so silly. She and I both wondered around all that time when there was a simple solution.

You know, life is like that. Stress can so overwhelm you in the moment trying to get to the next phase that you overlook a simple solution. I awoke to and clearly heard God was saying to me "Sweetie, you got to unpack your bag." My bag was little and red. Well, that represented my heart. There is all this stuff jammed in there that was stopping me from entering into my new, beautiful space and destination. Jammed packed in there was anger, resentment, bitterness, hurt, and rage, and well, I'd even say a touch of hate from all the hurt. There's insecurity from feeling left, older, and not enough of whatever we are supposed to be enough of. You name it! It was in there inside my heart.

How do you unpack your heart? Well, it's piece by piece;

examining the contents of your heart and then ask God to help you heal it. Sounds simple, right? Well, it is, and it isn't. The first thing to unpack is your pride. Then it gets easier from there.

Day 32

What things are in your heart that may stand in your way of moving on to a better beautiful space?

_____
_____
_____
_____
_____
_____
_____
_____
_____
_____
_____
_____

I'm grateful for :

_____
_____
_____
_____
_____
_____
_____
_____
_____
_____
_____
_____

Divine Meeting

Daily Dose

"If any of you lacks wisdom, you should ask God, who gives generously to all without finding fault, and it will be given to you."
James 1:5 (NIV)

Today I had a divine meeting that lasted three hours over breakfast. I got to share my passion for writing this book with an incredible lady who after her divorce had divine encounters that led her to become a best-selling author, attain several degrees, and live her life more abundantly. She could attest to the purpose for the pain, and this encourages me that there is a better life on the other side. Within a few minutes of our meeting, those very blessed words came out her mouth… the other side. God is coming for you. He is calling you to your calling. All you need to do is follow and answer, repeat. He is sending you a family of believers to rescue you and walk with you, and you will rescue and walk with another person coming behind you. We are all falling together, but we are also rising together too.

Day 33

What are you needing guidance on? Ask God to send the right people at the right time.

_____
_____
_____
_____
_____
_____
_____
_____

I'm grateful for these divine meetings:

_____
_____
_____
_____
_____
_____
_____
_____
_____
_____
_____
_____
_____
_____

Picture This

Daily Dose
"Love your neighbor as yourself."
Mark 12:31 (NIV)

    Today I want you to do something that will make you smile: take a selfie! Approximately 92 million selfies are taken every day. We have become a society that is attached to our phones, and capturing the moment to post online is a sacred event now. Why? You want to remember it to let others know you had it. Well, you may not fully know you even experienced it if you do not take a selfie of it, right? Lol! Well, not quite, but close.

    After the divorce, my ex tossed my pics off his Facebook, and I felt as if I had been deleted from his life which made me feel even more discarded. Certainly, there were not even that many on there because I think it showed what little value I had in his life as I look back. Nonetheless, he argued it was to help him "heal." It felt much more like "hiding" than an effort to "heal," but only he and God know the full truth. However, I came into my office space and felt his pictures no longer served me, worrying coworkers might look and say, "Oh, what a beautiful family or how long have you been married?" I dreaded these communication crises in which I would have inappropriately burst into tears. Therefore, I packed them up and left only the ones of my sons. As I looked around at the people I valued in frames, I felt someone had been neglected for some time - Me. I had left myself out my own life. So, I thought, well, starting now, I am going to put a pic of myself in here to remind myself I am loved too, and I deserve to appreciate myself. At first, I admit, it made me feel awkward, and I worried folks might think I was vain, so I slid it around behind my office phone, so only I could see it and then eventually on a table behind my desk in a more visible but not on mass display area.

Every time I looked at it, I was reminded to be available for myself. It was giving myself a one-minute pep talk or giving myself approval to step away and walk to visit a friend and coworker or even sip on a cup of comforting tea. Whatever it is that builds you up, do that. Now, use that handy phone and point it directly at your wonderful face and smile and then print it out. I sent mine to Walgreens and put it in a small frame. There I am every day looking at myself and reminding myself to value everyone in those frames. You are worth it; you deserve to value you.

Day 34

What ways might have you left yourself out the picture? Ask God to show you ways you can value yourself as He does.

___

I am grateful to have these qualities:

___

Moving Day

Daily Dose

"But Lot's wife looked back, and she became a pillar of salt."
Genesis 19:26 (NIV)

Have you ever moved from one place to another? If so then you know there will come a day that the moving truck will pull up and movers pack all your belongings, pack it in, and roll out to your next destination. This is often a mixed bag of emotions and truly a guaranteed exhausting day. It is the joining of an ending and a beginning. You mourn and rejoice all at once.

I recall the day my oldest was moving out and going to college. One moment, I was crying, and my husband would console me, and the next he was crying, and I would console him. The ride home was treacherous. We got into a horrible argument, and a bit of depression set in on both of us, and even our younger son had a tough time adjusting, too. You get through it and adjust, but change is not always rainbows and unicorns, even when you welcome it. Here is the thing: you need to plan a moving date. I mean an emotional moving date. You may part your items and things, but the contents of the hearts take years to part with.

I do not even know how to do this yet; I just hear the voice of God saying to let Him help you, so you do not keep looking back and become a pillar of salt. You are not meant to get stuck looking back at what was. You must keep going forward to what will be. Your future is so much better and brighter, and it is all that is left. Ahead, to the other side we go!

Day 35

What things, mindsets, habits, and even people do you need to move on from so you can go
where God is leading you?

_____
_____
_____
_____
_____
_____
_____
_____
_____
_____
_____
_____

I'm grateful to move on to these future
dreams and hopes:

_____
_____
_____
_____
_____
_____
_____
_____
_____

Locked Keys

Daily Dose
"And when you stand praying, if you hold anything against anyone, forgive them, so that your Father in heaven may forgive you your sins."
Mark 11:25 (NIV)

Oh, my goodness! We locked the keys inside the car! This is one of the most frustrating things that happens to travelers. You have a couple of options ... hope someone can go retrieve your spare set of keys if it is not too far from home, call a locksmith, or depending on the year of the vehicle, try to fenagle the lock with a coat hanger and get inside. None of the options are easy and quick retrieval methods. Working your way towards forgiveness is like that. It is often exceedingly difficult and brutal, and it leaves you stranded outside. You are unable to go anywhere mentally and emotionally free. The locks of anger and bitterness will not let you get in your own ride and go free. But, oh if you could just grab that key... That key is forgiveness that sets *you* free and not *them*. They are not even in the vicinity. They are no longer there held hostage by your emotions -only you are. Knowing that does not take away the feelings of unforgiveness, but it does show you that forgiveness is truly a gift to yourself, which makes you in turn want to achieve it rather than hold it back from the one who hurt you.

Thankfully, you have a master locksmith who is ready to help you open the door. Forgiveness does not allow continued mistreatment and does not require continued relationships. It is simply saying I am going to choose to not be locked outside with anger and bitterness wanting vengeance, and I am going to choose to trust God to right and wrong and heal me. They nor the enemy have no power over me.

Pray this prayer aloud. I forgive (name) for (offense), and I release them from this debt and receive God's healing and love in exchange as you forgive me of my debts. Amen. Forgiveness is a process, and you may need to repeat that prayer many times if you find yourself in pain or ruminating over the hurt. The point is not to just sit outside your goals and destiny but to actively ask God to help you and keep looking to move towards healing the hurt. Well, it looks as if the locksmith has arrived; now let us get those keys. You know where we are headed...yes, the other side!

Day 36

For what things has God forgiven you? What things do you need to forgive someone else?
Ask God to help you.

_____
_____
_____
_____
_____
_____
_____
_____
_____
_____

Forgiveness is a gift you give yourself.
How are you grateful to give this gift?

_____
_____
_____
_____
_____
_____
_____
_____
_____
_____
_____
_____
_____
_____

Casualties

Daily Dosage

"There is a time for everything and a season for every activity under the heavens."
Ecclesiastes 3:1 (NIV)

This may be the most difficult part of our journey. Aside from the broken relationship between you and your former spouse or loved one, I am going to prepare you may be more casualties. This is part of the departing: the parting of the bonded relationships you two may have shared together. It may be family, friends, and shared people who feel torn between the two of you who will feel a leaning to a loyalty of the one of you. It is okay. By that, I mean it is going to hurt, and you may need to mourn it also, but it is part of the process. There will also be a new you emerging and former friends and family who may have been just your own may now have to choose whether they embrace this new you and you may have to choose as well to embrace them as the new you. You will be told to not let it change you, but I say all of life every day we are changing just as the seasons change, as the leaves fall, and as all nature moves and shifts.

If it's alive, it changes. Inasmuch, there is the aging process proving itself evidence of every cell constantly changing, dying off, shedding, and rebuilding. Therefore, I say then it is not a matter of not changing but choosing how you will change. Some may see it for better and some for the worse, but it is important how God and you see it. I pray that each day you can look in the mirror and see a bit more of Him reflected in you. On to the other side we go, new you, old you, and all the parts in between.

Day 37

What relationships do you feel have changed/shifted?
Are these positive or negative shifts?

_____
_____
_____
_____
_____
_____
_____
_____
_____
_____

I am grateful to be growing and
changing in these ways:

_____
_____
_____
_____
_____
_____
_____
_____
_____
_____

Pay Attention

Daily Dose
*"Listen, my sons, to a father's instruction;
pay attention and gain understanding."*
Proverbs 4:1 (NIV)

Uh, oh...looks like we missed our turn. We got busy talking, and neither of us were paying attention. It happens. You know there is a reason it's called "paying" attention. It's because it costs you something, and when you do not do it, well, you lose something - in this case, a bit of lost time. Time is extremely valuable, and you can't get it back, but sometimes you can make up for it. One of the great wonders of God is He has the ability to redeem the time the enemy steals from you. Let's explore more significantly what can be really gained or lost. You!

Early on into my divorce process, I made some agreements with myself and with God.

1) God first
2) Then me

What I said to myself was, "God, You." I had not given myself enough attention. Often in a Christian society, we are praised for overlooking our needs, especially as women in society. We are told, take care of your kids, take care of your husband, your community, your mom, dad, brother, take care of everyone and everything, and somewhere near the bottom of the list if you make the list, ah...there is you. You, the insignificant, let it go; it is okay; it's not a big deal... you. Well, let me tell you what that thinking will get you: emptiness, a big hole of exhaustion, frustration, big ole bag of people pleasing nothing but anger and resentment. You must, I repeat, you must pay attention to yourself and your needs. Define them, ask for them to be met by those who want to and can, and for those who really do not want to and can't...they cannot have a lot of your energy. They just can't anymore. Why? They will end up overdrawing your account. You need people around you who you can deposit into your life, and you can deposit into theirs as well. I'm not saying every relationship has to be transactional at the heart of it but pay attention to those who give you energy and support you with being there emotionally, mentally, physically. Who calls you? Who comes to see you? Who replies and respects your boundaries and rises up without being asked all the time to be there? Who is not? You often find it's a one-way street that you keep doing all the driving down. Pay attention to these things and then respond appropriately. You are worth it! I repeat: you are worth it!

Day 38

Who is depositing into my life? Who is withdrawing more than they deposit? Ask God to reveal to you weeds and flowers in your life.
Trim the weeds and tend to the flowers.

___

I am grateful for these flowers:

Dating Yourself

Daily Dose
*"Be strong and take heart,
all you who hope in the* LORD.*"*
Psalm 31:24 (NIV)

I stumbled upon this concept on YouTube of all the most unlikely places. This beautiful YouTuber was there telling me to dress up and take myself out to dinner and go all the places I would enjoy going. Do not wait for someone else to take you. You know what - I decided to do just that. I was sick of sitting around the house on Friday night pining or crying, and my grieving was not always healthy in that way. I really looked forward to getting off early from work on Fridays, but I dreaded going home by myself to an empty house where my kids ran off to their own events, and my friends, well, they had their own lives with husbands and families, too. I didn't always want to be the planner of such events either. Therefore, a play at my college was a perfect opportunity to try such a date out. I bought the $15 tickets in advance, so I didn't back out and jazzed myself up. I did ask my son if he wanted to go, but he quickly declined, and off I went on my first self-date. Was I nervous that coworkers might say, "Hey, where's your husband?" I'd be lying to say that I did not have the dreaded, shamed feeling of divorce bubbling up. However, was I also excited to go to an event and do something I loved to do? Yes, I was even more so! Was this better than being home on my couch? Yes, absolutely! And you know what - I cleaned up good, and I fit right in the crowd. I sang that night. I cried with the actors. I dreamed and marveled at them. I even snuck away at intermission and enjoyed a pork sandwich, ate it behind the curtain, and sat in a different seat! I wouldn't have been able to do that with my ex in the past without drama.

You can enjoy your life all by yourself. You are complete all by yourself, and if you find someone who is just so fortunate to join you and compliments you in the future, well, that's just a cherry on top, but you are a whole bucket of ice cream all by yourself.

Day 39

Name a place or some places you can take yourself on a date. Plan it out here and go do it.

___

I'm grateful to have these qualities that
make me a good date:

___

Breathe

Daily Dose
"Then the LORD God formed a man from the dust of the ground and breathed into his nostrils the breath of life, and the man became a living being."
Genesis 2:7 (NIV)

Today I want you to breathe. One tool that has helped me along my journey is the Calm app. I came upon it right before my divorce, and like all other things it was an instrument God was just placing in His wonderful chorus that I would use to pick up and play when my heart was broken to help mend it and let me tell you how it did. It is a meditation app. Now, I am not much for that Zen life belief system, but I do know how important it is to slow down and just breathe. This app makes you do that and sends you daily different moderators to help guide you. Jay Shetty with his words of wisdom is one of my favorites. When I'd begun to feel stressed or overwhelmed with my thoughts, I'd pop on one of those sessions and focus only on the words of the person speaking on topics like mindfulness or gratitude. It never failed. God would weave in just what I needed to hear that day to keep me encouraged or challenged. However, my favorite part quickly became the part where I'd just focus on breathing in slowly and out slowly. It triggers your parasympathetic nervous system and makes you relax. It's telling you that you are safe!

Now, you try it. Lie down or sit in a comfortable space, preferably eyes closed, breathing in for count of eight, out for count of 11. Notice and pause in between breaths, and do not rush, just learn to relax and enjoy the process of relaxing well. Think: breathe in the good and out the bad. Life to my soul.

Day 40

Express how taking a moment to breathe made you feel. How might you incorporate breathing exercises into your day? (Bedtime, Morning, Drive to or from work?

_____
_____
_____
_____
_____
_____
_____
_____
_____
_____
_____
_____

I'm grateful to have these moments to breathe.

_____
_____
_____
_____
_____
_____
_____
_____

Offense

Daily Dose

"My dear brothers and sisters, take note of this: Everyone should be quick to listen, slow to speak and slow to become angry, because human anger does not produce the righteousness that God desires."
James 1:19-20 (NIV)

Today we are going to run over a fence. Yes, that's correct, a fence. We have been sitting on the edge of a fence way too long, and we keep falling off it and getting hurt repeatedly, so you know what, let's just rev up our engine and run the fence over. This way we will not let a fence get in our way any longer. I assume you get my play on words by now, "a fence," "offense." It is an easy place to find yourself once you've been hurt like we all feel, especially going through a challenging time like a divorce.

Offensive words and injurious behavior should not be excused and do not need to be defended; however, positioning yourself to be easily offended is another issue that can spring up from being wounded by someone you loved. You may find yourself in this position with everyone, not looking to be offended but more playing a blocking guard on a field, just looking to protect yourselves in the game of life. You are running plays constantly in your head, waiting to zig if they zag, and if they say this then I might say that, and if this happens then that. And the slightest tilt in the wrong direction, well, there you go in full-on attack mode, or you are on the field in pain calling for a stretcher to get you from the emotional pain. Let us rewind the tape. Just perhaps there was something deeper at root here that you misread the other player and there was not a foul on the field at all! Perhaps, they did choke-hold you and tackle you.

What are you going to do about it? You can lie there in pain or dust yourself off and go discuss the low hit. You can trust Jesus is the official on the field who does not miss any low blows, and he will flag it and rectify it. Ask Holy Spirit to help you not to be quickly offended and use wisdom to determine how to deal with true offenses. Sometimes we are to be still and know He is God; other times, we are challenged to confront. Either way, we never walk in fear which is often the culprit behind living in constant offense, fearing more hurt.

Day 41

What are some offenses you have experienced during this time in your life? What are some healthy ways to resolve them?

_____
_____
_____
_____
_____
_____
_____
_____
_____
_____
_____
_____
_____
_____

Gratitude cancels out a spirit of Offense.
Let's be grateful for these 5 things today:

_____
_____
_____
_____
_____
_____
_____
_____
_____
_____
_____

Open Road

Daily Dose

*"I will go before you
and will level the mountains;
I will break down gates of bronze
and cut through bars of iron."*
Isaiah 45:2 (NIV)

This morning on my drive to work, there was an unexpected praise day of joy due to an open road! You see the overpass on my way to work had been under construction for at least two years, and it had caused everyone to have to loop around and detour and go through a maze of confusing orange cones and zones. As soon as you got used to it, they would change it up as the road construction progressed, and just this week it changed so drastically, I got stuck and wasn't sure which lane to enter safely. The car behind me began honking their horn in frustration, anxiety cranked up, and then a bit of anger as I proceeded with caution praying that I was not heading into oncoming traffic. I edged forward and quickly moved right into the lane I needed to safely get to my destination all the while saying a few words under my breath for the person behind me and the whole situation. Nevertheless, what a difference a few days make!

Today as I moved on to the same roadway, the path was made clear. The cones were still there, but they were in a straight line, and I no longer had to maneuver them like Mario Andretti. I just rolled with ease to the right and glided on freely. I turned down my praise music on the radio and made my own joyful noise to God. I began all out jigging, shoulder-bouncing, head-bopping crazy lady car dancing and hollering and shouting, "Hey, yeah! Thank you, God!"

As I rolled up the workers, God laid it on my heart to roll down my windows and thank them for their arduous work. So, I did! I said, "Thank you for all your hard work. I am so glad this road is finally open. I'm saying Thank you God!" The guys just smiled, nodded, waved, and said, "You're welcome! Have a good day." These fellas had been out there working all the while in the scorching, dangerous triple digit heat, rain, freezing cold for years, preparing the way - sweating, freezing, sometimes sick, tired, away from family and loved ones, making a minimum wage at that. Some might say, well, they are just doing their job; true, but that does not mean doing their job did not benefit many other people. You see, it is time to recognize when people who are behind the scenes "just doing their job" are helping pave the way for you. Tell them thanks. There are so many people God is and has and will continue to place in your life through challenges, especially like divorce. If you just look, you will see they are paving the roadway. Don't just ride on to the other side and do not just praise God. Stop, roll down the window, look them in the eye, and tell them thank you!

Day 42

Who has helped pave the road to the other side for you?
Ask God to reveal them. It may even be your ex.
List them here, screenshot, text them and tell them in your words:
Thank you.

_____
_____
_____
_____
_____
_____
_____
_____
_____
_____
_____
_____
_____
_____

I'm so grateful for these people who are helping me to get to the other side.

_____
_____
_____
_____
_____
_____
_____
_____
_____
_____
_____

Untying Soul Ties

Daily Dose

"Do you not know that he who unites himself with a prostitute is one with her in body? For it is said, 'The two will become one flesh.'"
1 Corinthians 6:16 (NIV)

The first time I heard of a soul tie was from a friend from my Divorce Care class. I thought, *hmm, what*? Wait, are you talking about that Disney movie, *Soul*? No, not at all, but sort of all at the same time. In the movie, the lost soul goes drifting out into oblivion as it is tied to its purpose and this other entity as they both embark on a journey together to get back to earth to fulfill it together. In that sense, I'd say that is a soul tie. For some people, it is good to be tied to but others not so much. It will feel like a chain gang most days. They sometimes drain you emotionally, mentally, physically, and financially and leave you all out depleted. These ones, you need to untie yourself from. It can be hard even after the divorce though. You will find yourself caught in the pain, the words spoken over you, the hurt or wondering what happened if it might have turned out differently. None of this will do you any good.

    I challenge you today to do one of the hardest things yet: unfollow and unfriend. Untie and unburden yourself of the idea that you must be connected in any way in any shape in any form whatsoever. I do not care if you are parents, grandparents, or any of it. You must take ownership of your relationship with your children and not allow them to manage it period. It's broken for a reason, but you no longer have to be broken with it. Untie yourself from what is broken and begin to heal yourself in an incredible, scary, yes, but most healthy way. Do what only the brave can do and some take years to do: untie now. Do not be forever attached to someone who no longer wants to be attached to you.

Day 43

Do you have a soul-tie that needs to be broken?
Ask God to reveal any to you and the power to pray and receive freedom.

_____
_____
_____
_____
_____
_____
_____
_____
_____
_____
_____
_____
_____
_____
_____

Express your gratitude here:

_____
_____
_____
_____
_____
_____
_____
_____
_____
_____
_____
_____
_____
_____

Alignment

Daily Dose

*"Now you are the body of Christ,
and each one of you is a part of it."*
1 Corinthians 12:27 (NIV)

Alignment! I have heard this phrase all over the place, but it never quite clicked until today. I was listening to a message about how complaining is a curse; the pastor referenced how complaining is most often done in a pack, and it is like a disease because it spreads through your alignment or your group. Therefore, you must get in the correct alignment.

After my car wreck, one ache led to another ache until I found myself at a chiropractor. As I waited, I stared at a diagram of the spine on the wall. It showed how every nerve running along the spinal vertebrae led to a certain area of our body, and if that vertebra was out of alignment, it led to all kinds of ailments. Judging from the diagram, I read internally, migraines, check, insomnia, check, blood pressure, check, yep…looks like C1 might be my area. Well, when the x-rays and examinations were complete, sure enough C1 was clearly out of alignment, or as I had rather put it, simply jacked up! No wonder, you have pain, no rest, no flow, no ease, and so it is, when you are not in alignment and you find yourself with some old toxic thoughts, toxic behaviors, beliefs and yes, even people, some family, some friends, ouch that hurt, but it is true, and you have just got to be willing to step away and go be alone with God and ask him to realign you.

Especially for those who can be a people pleaser like me, God wants you to find your voice and your trust in Him. It is going to challenge old friendships and old everything. Look out for quick fixes but prayerfully and carefully step away. Be willing to let it all go so God can tear down anything that is crippling you from growing close to Him. Shut out every single voice but His. I do mean, every single one, the ones that use to give you direction, the ones that shout, and the ones that whisper and seem right. His voice is duplicated in His word because He is the Word. You are going to have to read and pray and then do it again, and it will show up in other ways, but first start with His word and prayer. This is not a lazy man's work, but I promise neither is it a lazy man's profit. It will yield a great reward on the other side.

Day 44

Looking at your social circle, how might you need to adjust your alignment? Sometimes you need to put the right people in the right places; others season may be over.
Ask God now and write down what names of those He reveals.

_____
_____
_____
_____
_____
_____
_____
_____
_____
_____
_____
_____
_____
_____
_____
_____
_____

I am grateful for all who have played a role in my life. Here's how some have helped me grow:

_____
_____
_____
_____
_____
_____
_____
_____
_____
_____
_____

Broken for Better

Daily Dosage
"He heals the broken heart and binds up the wounds."
Psalm 147:3 (NIV)

And so, as the vow is written, for better or worse. Well, here we are now, the vow has been broken. Now what? Well, I say broken for better. You will not see it right now perhaps or maybe you do. There are days that I see the light peeking through the clouds, and I can predict warm weather ahead and sunshine, and it looks so much better. I click on my bank account, and I feel a little more financially secure. I have more energy, and yes, I even do believe I laughed today. I laughed a lot, and I even got hit on. There's newness in the air. I have made new friends and have new places to go, and my home is even feeling less like it was before. This is your opportunity to look around and find what is better. Often, the marriage was sick, so the symptoms were there long before the divorce. That is not to say one party did not bring in the bulk of the disease or not, or the illness was short lived, and then the relationship quickly died. Nonetheless, it was clearly broken, ill and not working; otherwise, you would still be together. By that same token, many marriages are still together that are malignant and cancerous. Together does not equal thriving either. Now, it is over, and it's broken, and just like a bone, you can reset. You can be molded, mended, and become better and stronger. You will need to mobilize your injury, take delicate care of it, and shield it from more harm, but you will heal. Given the proper care and time, you will be able to fully use your injured heart to its full capacity and love again.

Day 45

Name some ways in which you see that your life is better. Look for the good and you will find it.

___

I look forward to these things today:

This Is a Test

Daily Dose
*"Search me, God, and know my heart;
test me and know my anxious thoughts."*
Psalm 139:23 (NIV)

I recall as a child before the age of streaming TV, back when there were only about 5 major channels, every now and then the TV station would run a test. It would display a color bar and play an annoying constant beeping sound. Meanwhile, a man's boring stern voice would state repeatedly, "This is test. This is only a test brought to you by your broadcasting station." It would last about a minute or two or so. However, to a child eagerly awaiting to return to my morning cartoon of *Bugs Bunny: and Wile E. Coyote*, it seemed like forever. I am like, come on already! And just when I had run out of patience, the ever so boring man's voice would come back on and state, "This concludes the test; you may now return to your regularly scheduled programming."

All of life is like that, whether you are stuck in traffic, trying your best not to curse and blow the horn and yell, get out the way - a patience test, it may be a more difficult test - a prolonged illness, or in our case, a divorce. We are all just waiting to get back to regularly scheduled programming, the thing we call daily life that is comfortable or at least semi-comfortable. The tests will come, but you can think of this and think of the voice as God's. It is not stressed; it is calmly saying...It is only a test...it's concluded, but He does not just want to take you back to regularly scheduled programming. He wants to grow you to pass the test and arrive on the other side. Smile and get ready for your debut!

Day 46

List some ways you have been tested.
Pray and ask God how to handle these.
Repent if you fail and move forward. It is ok.
Often, you even get another chance to retest.

___

What things are you grateful to have learned from life's test?

Scar Tissue

Daily Dose
"From now on, let no one cause me trouble, for I bear on my body the marks of Jesus."
Galatians 6:17 (NIV)

"That is going to leave a scar!" It is not something anyone wants to hear, but it's true. Trauma leaves scars. Unlike physical ones on the outside from blunt force, emotional ones are internal, but they have hit your core with even more catastrophic force. It's just no one sees it - not really. Well, they may see the manifestation of pain, which shows up in all kinds of ways.

    I recall having a hysterectomy due to fibroid tumors and years of a heavy menstrual cycle that left me with fatigue and anemia. After the surgery, I recall the doctor telling me the procedure had taken him much longer than planned because I had so much internal scar tissue from my two previous c-sections. He said the scar tissue had bonded itself to my other organs, and he had to wrestle with it to get it free.

    Here's the thing: divorce comes with scars. You may have to wrestle with them and the damage they cause to get free, so you can heal and function better. Notice, I said better. Perfection is a lie! No one is walking around 100% healed, no trauma, skipping through the lilies. And if they tell you they are, they just lied to cover up something they can't handle mentally. Anyhow, go to the source and get your healing. Also, do practical things like seek out therapy. I started therapy before my divorce and sought marriage and personal counseling many times. I believe in therapy. I read books. I do the work, even when it gets hard, when no one sees, when I cry, and when I want to give up and sometimes, I do give up, and then I come back and begin again. This is wrestling. You are fighting with yourself for a better you. Keep fighting. We are going to the other side.

Day 47

You cannot heal what you conceal. Be free to list what you have been wrestling with below. God is ready to heal. Scars are signs that a wound has healed.

List ways you feel grateful for the scars you have:

Nature Walk

Daily Dose
*"For since the creation of the world God's invisible qualities—his eternal power and divine nature—
have been clearly seen, being understood from what has been made, so that people are without excuse."*
Romans 1:20 NIV

It's time to park the car and go on a nature walk. This morning, God sent me on a nature walk. The first thing He had me to do was pick up an acorn and walk with it. As I did while looking all around in nature and saw Him, the song "God Will Work It Out" by Maverick City came through my earphones. "Before I knew my name, before I drew a breath, He was making ways for me. Now and every day, in each and every step."

I marveled at the trees and saw Him in the stems in the leaves, the pebbles in the stream, and the flow of the birds above in the cotton candy blue sky. There He is - everywhere! I walked this park so many times, but He was never more present. So it is, you are going about your daily routines, sometimes walking, running, by yourself or alongside a friend, a stranger that walks by, nods, and says, "Good morning." He is all around everywhere, whether you know it or not. Be reminded He put the whole earth together. He will and is putting you back together. Healing is happening whether you know it or not.

Get out in nature today. Look for something to pick up and take back or take a picture of it and then research it. I guarantee you will see God in it, and it will provide some healing to you.

Day 48

In what park or neighborhood can you stroll today?
How did His creation speak to you?

___

Today, I am grateful for these things in creation:

Open Your Mouth

Daily Dose

"A good man brings good things out of the good stored up in his heart, and an evil man brings evil things out of the evil stored up in his heart.
For the mouth speaks what the heart is full of."
Luke 6:45 (NIV)

Today I had to take an x-ray. The tech was so enjoyable to talk to, I did not even mind the awkward poses I had to get into to get the images. He and I often share our interest in writing and creative passions, and I feel as if I am pouring into a nephew, which is extremely rewarding as an encourager. One such pose requires you to open your mouth while you stand still, and a bright light is shining down your throat to get a good image of your spine connecting to the base of your brain and skull.

Much of your healing will require you to stand still and open your mouth and expose what is on the inside. It needs to have a light shone on it. No one can say it for you. You cannot just pray it away. You must open wide and speak it - the hurt; the pain; the need; the confession; all of it must be said. Sometimes, crying out, and I do mean yelling into the heavens with all the anguish and pain inside of you coming out and giving it to Him is releasing it. Other times, you need to express it directly to the people who have hurt you or you have hurt. Ask God for the wisdom to know the difference and for the timing and words to do it and if and when to do it. If He leads you to do it, do not be afraid. He has not given you a spirit of fear.

It's yours to say, don't let anyone silence you with religion or guilt. Say it. Own it. That is the only way you get free. The truth should make you free.

Day 49

What is inside you that is and has been causing you anguish and pain that needs to be expressed?

How can you honor yourself and give it a voice? Write a letter? Scream it out to God? Go to that person and discuss it? Or maybe it's all of the above. Your healing is on the other side. Go get it.

Rest Stop

Daily Dose

*"Come to me, all you who are weary and burdened,
and I will give you rest."*
Matthew 11:28 (NIV)

    This may be the most important stop of our journey. The Rest Stop is usually sitting off the highway with easy access allowing you to pull off at the interstate and take a much-needed break before you fall asleep behind the wheel. You need a potty break; either way, mother nature is calling you one way or another and telling you...hey, it's time - time to STOP, here and NOW. You may not get another chance before it's too late, and you've soiled your britches as mom says, or God forbid, the church head nod has begun, and you're swerving off the road. Therefore, take the clues from your body, use your brain, and pull off the road.

    No one can fully function without proper rest. Grief has a funny way of showing up in each of us. Sometimes you may feel like running, so you don't have to think about the pain and sorrow. Other times you may want to just sit there and drown in your sorrow. Neither of the two allows for rest. Rest is a place of knowing God's got it under control, and your body and mind are at peace because of it.

    Consider Jesus sleeping on the boat while the disciples were stressing out about the storm. That's what rest really looks like. Jesus was not pulling the ropes to the sails among them and working; neither was He down in the lower parts crying out with sorrow. He was fast asleep: resting.

Take today to seek, rest, and be nourished, knowing God has every storm in your life under control. If it's warm out today, go lie in the grass and look up for a moment; if not, find a spot in your home, on a park bench, or in your bed even and really focus on resting in knowing God will calm the storm. Pull in now and let's rest because you know where we are headed, my friend: the other side.

Day 50

Make a plan for rest. Write it here:

I am grateful for rest. List ways it helps you restore.

Road to Repentance

Daily Dose

"Therefore, confess your sins to each other and pray for each other so that you may be healed. The prayer of a righteous person is powerful and effective."
James 5:16 (NIV)

    Even if you feel you did everything you could have to make it work, there is always something that will trip you up and make you think: *what if...this or I regret that, saying this, thinking that, doing this, saying that if only had I not. Or this and that...You made mistakes.* Some you might consider catastrophic, unforgivable even, but God does not. He knows them all, yet He loves you and is waiting for you to come and confess them to Him. He is ready to forgive and help you move forward. He is ready to free you from your sin and unforgiveness. Whether it's the unforgiveness you feel towards your ex-spouse or the unforgiveness you feel towards yourself, either way it's a personal prison. The wardens are named Guilt, Shame, and Punishment. They are determined to keep you locked in that cell looking for a way to earn your way out or pay the unpurchaseable price for the other person's freedom. Along comes Hatred and Bitterness, and they stand at the door of your heart and keep out all the good too, locking you inside an even lonelier place.
    Give the key over to God in prayer. It is a process much like selling a home. First, you recognize you need to relocate and need new surroundings, so you prepare your surroundings for a new owner, and you entertain new buyers where you open your home to viewers, and you come to an agreement, and finally the sale is made for a fair price. Here is the best part with God. He owns all the real estate! He has so much more in store! Let it all go. Turn the key over to Him and watch what happens.

Day 51

List and pray over the things you feel you need to repent. God is waiting to restore you.

_____
_____
_____
_____
_____
_____
_____
_____
_____
_____
_____
_____
_____

I am grateful for the forgiveness I received.
Being forgiven made me feel:

_____
_____
_____
_____
_____
_____
_____
_____
_____
_____
_____

Wreckage

Daily Dose

*"The beginning of wisdom is this: Get wisdom.
Though it cost all you have, get understanding."*
Proverbs 4:7 (NIV)

Here is the thing. After a divorce, there is often a lot of wreckage. Depending on how long you were together, there may be tons to dig yourself out of emotional, mental, physical, and financial wreckage. Truth be told, you may be digging yourself out for some time to come, even years. It is okay. Rome wasn't built in a day, and you are way more beautiful and brilliant than Rome, so every brick you lay in paving your future is worth it.

There are some things to consider that may hurt, but you should not be afraid to examine and look for truth. Ask God to reveal these things to you as you read over these potential pitfalls just so you can establish a fundamental truth. Truth is so important because it will direct your future. I came to terms with some of these things, and it helps me to continually choose not to forever mourn the loss of my marriage.

You must get clear on what happened and why. I do not believe you can truly heal and move forward on the premise of "Well, I don't understand, but it's okay." I think deep within us is a yearning for truth, an explanation. Now the tricky part is, it is easy to make up a reason and live a lie, but that's just the problem with saying I don't know, and it's okay. You will internally constantly turn the potential reasons over in your head and heart until you come up with some type of answer, or you will sink into a depression of leaving yourself.

Do not throw yourself away! I repeat do not throw yourself away! Ask the tough questions. Seek and you will find. Pray and find understanding, peace, forgiveness, and equip yourself for the future to open new doors, so you don't walk into another relationship making some of the same mistakes.

Perhaps your marriage was not ordained by God... that's why it led to a destructive life and one of hurt. It may have been designed for a season. Yes, I said it and meant it. Some relationships are there for a season, including marriages, just like all relationships. People change and so do relationships. Who you marry will not be the same person in about five years after that because we are forever changing. Both parties must be committed to having a relationship and putting in a fair amount of reciprocity for it to function well. Otherwise, they simply disintegrate. I know God has designed marriages He helps put together to last, but the free will He gives us is still and always operating.

Other questions to ask:

Did you have...
- Emotional physical mental union connection
- Partnering with purpose
- Healthy boundaries
- God as head
- Suitable mate - a friendship
- Warfare
- Submission
- Idolatry

Arrival

Daily Dose

"Therefore, there is now no condemnation for those who are in Christ Jesus, because through Christ Jesus the law of the Spirit who gives life has set you free from the law of sin and death."
Romans 8: 1-2 (NIV)

At last, we have arrived! Well, we have at least come from one place to another, and my hope and prayer is that along our journey together, you have grown. Here's the thing I didn't tell you in the beginning. It's a one-way trip. Yes, there is no returning home. You do not get to go back to the place you came from. It's no longer there. Do you recall in the beginning as we set out on our road trip that I urged us to focus on the future and in looking back you would become a pillar of salt? Well, that place you came from does not exist anymore. It's part of the wreckage, and it got burned up in the fire. Meanwhile, here's the other thing, the most valuable and irreplaceable things you took with you! You still have them, and you are going to settle into a new place with all the things you really need.

What is with you? It is more of knowing that Jesus is there and a complete reliance on Him. He is helping you to establish self-confidence again and boundaries. He is bringing you into alignment with other believers and restoring your heart to forgive and look for healthy relationships with yourself and others. Why would you return to a burnt down house when you can build something beautiful and new? Am I saying no one should ever reconcile? Absolutely not! However, you better let God reveal to you if that's what He wants and not just yourself. I am saying, do not stay in sorrow, pain, or judgement or waiting for people to change but walk forward in your future trusting God is with you and He has set you free from your past. God wants all his children free.

    He spoke this revelation to me on top of a roof at a restaurant one night on a date with myself as I looked out over a crowd of people enjoying time with friends and family. They were listening to music, laughing, and having a good time. I thought how He must look down and see us with love and think I want you all to be free. In that moment, I felt myself allowing unforgiveness to leave me and unburden me. Yes, He wants us to free our debtors, people who have hurt us, so the devil does not have a foothold to bring havoc into our lives: free from sin and the jail it puts us in; free to love ourselves and others; free to live life fully and with joy. Just free!

Conclusion

I enjoyed riding with you. There is no other place I would have rather been than by your side. Email me at othersidedivorce@gmail.com and tell me how this book has helped you get to The Other Side.

_____
_____
_____
_____
_____
_____
_____
_____
_____
_____
_____
_____

    I leave you with my thoughts of gratitude. I'm grateful to have been here with you each day. I am thankful that God doesn't waste our pain and He really does give us beauty for ashes. It has been a long-time dream of mine to become an author, and through my biggest adversity in life, He birthed a dream. It is for more than me; it is for me and you. And, so it is for you as well. Your pain is not just for your healing but others as well. Get healed, and then go out and heal the sick, the broken-hearted, and tell them about Jesus. I love you.

Notes and Reflections

About the Author

My name is Felisha Gail Taylor, maiden name Fowler. I was married for 23 years, and shortly after my divorce, God reignited my passion for writing. He spoke to me about writing a divorce devotional to help others, especially women who are going through such a difficult time in life. I want everyone who is experiencing the pain of a divorce to know that you are not alone. Moreover, all things do really work for your good. All events can lead you to the other side.

During my journey, I battled all the events in this book from depression, anger, hurt, and confusion. I still feel the presence of these but much less and with a renewed sense of peace now. I know without a doubt that there is an "other side", and you are meant to head towards it.

While I'm not a counselor, I pray the tools I picked up along my journey can serve you well. I also encourage you to seek medical attention, a mental therapist, and physical and spiritual tools and put them in action. We are multi-faceted beings, and we need multi-faceted tools to operate well.

I enjoyed our journey, and I thank you for riding with me and letting me ride with you during this very private and tough time. May you feel the wind in your hair and cheek to let it remind you it's a kiss of God each time. See you on the other side!

www.ingramcontent.com/pod-product-compliance
Lightning Source LLC
Chambersburg PA
CBHW071117160426
43196CB00013B/2604